The House of Black and White

The House of Black and White

My Life with and Search for Louise Johnson Morris

By

David Sherer

Strategic Book Publishing and Rights Co.

Strategic Book Publishing and Rights Co.
12620 FM 1960, Suite A4-507
Houston TX 77065
www.sbpra.com

ISBN: 978-1-62857-521-7

Dedication

ಶಿೀಲ

For Louise, Chester, and Christopher (whom I never knew)

Acknowledgments

ॐ

This book has been more than two and a half years in the making. It has been quite gut-wrenching at times, and on many occasions, for varying reasons, I felt I should have thrown in the towel. Although I feel, in some respects, that this is a "risky" book to write, thankfully, I persevered. This "risk" comes in offending family, the black community, and members of my own faith. My intention is to tell a story so personal and with themes so central to who I am that I am willing to takes these risks. My last intention is to offend.

There have been many people crucial to its creation. First, I would like to thank Chester Lee Morris, Louise Johnson Morris's son, for his time and energy in sharing whatever information he had about his life with and without his mother by his side. Thanks also to the entire Johnson family ~ each and every one ~ of Macon, Georgia, Louise's hometown, where I was treated like family.

I would be remiss not to mention the gracious hospitality of Dr. Thomas R. Flynn, distinguished professor of philosophy at Emory University, for his continuing friendship and support and for being my host on my many trips to Atlanta. Gratitude is due Diane Hull, LCSW-C, as well, for her insights and wisdom. Photographer Rick Waldroup has my thanks for his kind sharing of information about the Baker Hotel in Mineral Wells, Texas.

No amount of gratitude can express my reliance and tribute to my excellent editor, Tracy Quinn McLennan, whose oversight of the project has made it, I feel, a worthy work. I'd also like to thank Bill Adler, Jr., a fellow writer and friend, for introducing me to Tracy. I would like to thank my outstanding cover designer, Kim Abraham, for putting a creative and artistic face to this work. My brother, Daniel, has been of enormous help, both for his brilliant and creative Archives as well as his literary and artistic insights.

Thanks go out to my mother, Leah L. Sherer, who shared stories and ideas concerning the dynamics of our family. Though we don't always see eye to eye, her tales of older times give color and completeness to the work. I hope that she agrees we have achieved a "state of grace."

To those who have cheered me on these few years by Facebook, in person, and by other means, I say, "Thank you, all." You know who you are. Gratitude is due, as well, to author Gary Krist for his helpful advice. Thank you to my excellent publishing team at SBPRA and to steadfast childhood friends, Stephen F. Dejter, Jr., MD; Michael Kolker; Lee Burgunder; and Richard Carroll.

Finally, thanks Laura, Liam, and Bangles for sticking with me.

Table of Contents

ℰℐℭℬ

Epigraph

ᏯᏆ

Both read the bible day and night,
but thou read'st black where I read white.

William Blake
1757-1827

Introduction

∞ఴ

The name "Bethesda" comes from the Bible. With origins in both Aramaic and Hebrew, it literally means "house of mercy" or "house of grace." It is also where the Bible states miracles occurred; the lame were healed there as the angels swirled the waters in the "Pool of Bethesda." Its significance can be considered twofold: It was both a place of disgrace, owing to the collection of invalids who came there, and a place of grace, where the unwell came and were made well.

Bethesda, Maryland, a thriving and bustling suburb of Washington, DC, is where I spent most of my childhood between 1962 and 1976. Louise Johnson Morris, the African American woman whose life is the center of this work, lived with my family all of those years.

Our house was truly one of duality – a house of mercy and pain, a place of joy and sorrow, a house most certainly of black and white.

Foreword

༚

The granddaughter of slaves, Louise Johnson (later she added "Morris" to her name after her second marriage) was born in Macon, Georgia on March 10th, 1922. She lived a long and challenging life under extraordinarily difficult times in our country for people like her. Like thousands of African American women of her generation, she courageously left her home to find out about the world, make a living, and perhaps to find a life's mate and have a family. She also learned much about herself. Little did she know that she would become ~ for me and many who knew her ~ a great teacher. Her common sense, humor, knowledge of the Bible, warmth, work ethic, and sense of self-sacrifice made her many friends and admirers.

In the almost twenty-two years that I knew Louise, she became indispensable to my overall development, sense of self, and even emotional health. She lived with our family during highly charged and unusual times, and her interactions with our friends and neighbors left them with a biding affection for her. Even these many years later, the mere mention of her name to people who knew her evokes an automatic smile.

In the course of creating this work, it has been a challenge to piece together Louise's past due to a multitude of factors, including scant documentation, incomplete oral history by family members, and a paucity of recollections by any of her friends and acquaintances. Nonetheless, I have done my utmost with the materials I had at hand.

This memoir is an homage to her and a catharsis of sorts for me. Though memory can be faulty, all of it is true, at least from my perspective.

A note on language: In every instance in which I quote Louise's pronunciation, syntax, and general use of her version of English, I quote it verbatim. I have used my best attempt to transcribe the sound of her use of the language, and no disrespect, prejudice, or any other form of denigration is implied or intended. *Her speech represented in this work appears exactly as I heard, and remember, it.*

Some of the language in this work is harsh. I mean not to offend but to present the story as accurately as possible.

Chapter One

The "Home-House"

∞∞

Macon, Georgia

Spring 1937

Fifteen-year-old Louise Johnson is toiling in the morning sun. It is late spring of 1937, and the heat and humidity have come too early and ferociously even for this part of Georgia. The massive wooden plow, hitched to the straining mule, forces Louise to push harder, deeper as the stubborn southern soil yields to the blade. Most of her siblings are still asleep, a fact that endears her even more to her father, Thomas, the son of slaves. (Decades later, she would boast to me how she was her father's favorite out of his ten children. She had always taken pride in telling me that she was the hardest working.) She pulls an old kerchief from her pocket and wipes the salty sweat from her face. Blowing the air from her cheeks, she puts the wadded cloth back into her shirt and resumes her work on land rendered more than seventy years earlier as reparations for the evil that was slavery.

Twenty years later, in Washington, DC, I am born into a strikingly different family and surroundings. The firstborn male with two older sisters, I come into the world with parents who are Jewish, well-schooled in the healing professions, and poised to improve their social standing. My ancestors, the world's most read book says, were slaves in another place and time. That story would be immortalized in painting, opera, literature, poetry, and other high art. The story of southern slavery in the U.S. was just catching up.

Eventually, the intersection of Louise's life with that of my family will change them all, but it is I who will be affected the most.

In the spring of 2012, after our separation of thirty-one years, I will watch with sadness as Louise's remains are lowered into the Georgia soil, adjacent to her parents' and a mere mile or two from where she pushed that plow.

Chapter Two

House of Peace

୫୦୯ଃ

**Silver Spring, Maryland and Somerset, Maryland
1959-1962**

My first memories of Louise are vague. She stands off to the left, a figure quietly shifting above the kitchen sink, with her back to me. From where I could just rest my dribbling eighteen-month-old chin on the cold bar of the crib, it could not have been more than ten feet. The faint but distinct waft of menthol from the Noxema she used every day hung in the air. Until the time we moved from middle-class Silver Spring to sylvan and idyllic Somerset, not much more appears in my mind of her. No touch of ebony skin, no apron to bury a forehead ~ just a few of the things that I would come to associate with Louise as I got a little older.

But all that changed. By the time I was two, the rambler in Somerset with the weeping willow tree, back porch, and lone swing was the perfect place for a growing mind. Somerset was everything the name implied. A hamlet of green wedged firmly between racially and religiously restrictive Kenwood, aristocratic Chevy Chase, and the Northwest DC line with enough trees, flowers, and thick grass to bury a child's chin smile-deep. (No blacks or Jews were allowed to live in communities of "restrictive covenants.") My father, Max, was in his first years of medical practice, having completed his fellowship in endocrinology at the prestigious National Institutes of Health in Bethesda, Maryland. My mother, Leah, a former operating room nurse, was busy tending to her children. The oldest, Deborah, was five years old and Lisa was three and a half. Since my father was almost always working, I found myself surrounded by females except for our dog King, a boxer-pointer mix. My sisters spent their days during the school year at Somerset Elementary, so I was left with my mom and Louise in the house much of the time. But it was Louise, more than my mother or anyone else in my life at the time, who would eventually shape whatever ego-strengthening views of myself I could muster. Her presence would also make an indelible mark on the way I eventually saw the world.

Years later, my mother told me that Louise came to us from a notice in *The Washington Post*. "A-Number-One Maid Needed!" it shouted. Mom felt she needed help raising the kids, especially Lisa who had hearing and behavioral problems, so she and my father placed the ad. Louise arrived at our home on Colston Drive in Silver Spring. The two women took a liking to each other, and she was hired on the spot.

###

This scene played out commonly in those days in DC. Young black women, having no real chance for advancement or any semblance of a professional life, joined families as domestics, becoming cooks, nurse maids, house cleaners, and, for a want of a better term, servants. This arrangement between a young black woman and an upwardly mobile Jewish family was nothing unusual for the time and was so meaningful for me when the film *Driving Miss Daisy* came along decades later.

For so many poor blacks of the time, the massive migration north from cities like Atlanta, Birmingham, Jackson, and Wilmington meant work, money, and possibly a better life. The District of Columbia of the 1960s held an atypical place in the list of cities that absorbed these immigrants. Unlike Boston, New York, Detroit, or Philadelphia, Washington was, in many ways, more southern than northern. Although the nation's capital and seat of the federal government, DC was south of the Mason-Dixon line and separated from the capital of the Confederacy, Richmond, by little more than 100 miles. Gettysburg, where so many were slaughtered those hot few days in July almost a century before, lay equidistant to the north. The only physical barrier that split DC off from the South was the Potomac River, but the cultural divide between the two was often as narrow as the river's width at Chain Bridge. Culturally, Washington was more genteel than Cleveland, more aristocratic than Chicago, and less provincial than Boston. It was in many ways, however, as segregated as Savannah or Mobile. Blacks still had separate restrooms and drinking fountains and could not sit at the lunch counter at People's Drugs on Wisconsin Avenue in DC or Maryland. They could not swim at the famous Crystal Pool at Glen Echo Amusement Park where the whites cooled themselves after rides in the bumper cars, trying their luck at the shooting gallery, or getting their weight guessed by the carnival barker.

The Washington that my mother and I knew, despite our being Jewish, was quite different. Passable as non-Jews in the often racially and religiously restricted environment of the time, we freely moved in circles where women wore white gloves between Memorial Day and Labor Day, and men commonly wore white bucks and lightweight fedoras in summer. Our life in Somerset was unique in that it was the only time I can recall my mother being consistently happy. It was there, also, that the images and influences of Louise ~ or "Weezy" as we started to call her ~ took permanent hold of me. Unfortunately, the interaction between my mother and Louise, at that point in my life, remains a virtual blank.

While my sisters were in school at Somerset Elementary, Mom spent her days studying modern dance, practicing the piano, grocery shopping, gassing up the family station wagon, getting clothes for the kids, and ferrying Lisa to various doctors and behavioral specialists. I would accompany her on some of these excursions, and a big treat for me was grabbing lunch at the Hot Shoppes (one of the many creations of the early Marriott Corporation) on the corner of Wisconsin Avenue and East West Highway in Bethesda's epicenter. Coffee was served in white china cups with saucers by waitresses (most of them were Caucasian but a smattering of blacks held the coveted job) wearing hairnets, caps, starched uniforms with cuffed short sleeves, and white shoes. Cream for the coffee came in small glass bottles with paper tab tops. My mother would lunch on egg salad sandwiches with fries and coffee. I happily ordered a hot dog and a Coke or an orange freeze served with shaved ice in a contoured glass. I wondered why the waitresses would ask if we wanted our Coke served "with or without ammonia" (a common practice at the time for "health reasons"). If we were in a hurry, we would sit at the counter where the frigid linoleum counter would allow me a vigorous forearm push-off to spin around 360 degrees on the orange, patent leather-covered swivel chair. From that vantage point, I could spy the diners down the line: business men in suits and ties, construction workers in heavy leather belts and scratched hard hats, moms with other kids, and young, pretty, lipsticked secretaries out for a quick lunch.

My mother and I would wait for the school bus to drop off my two older sisters every day after school. We would sit by the fire hydrant on Dorset Avenue in Somerset naming each car that drove by. Each correct guess earned a delicate pinch on my earlobe from my mom. Every time I pass that same hydrant this half century later my mind's ear hears "Chevrolet, I pinch your ear."

Compared to the middle and later years of her adult life, my mother was a different person in those days. Born in New York City in 1928, she and her mother, Hannah, soon left the United States for what was then Palestine in the early 1930s, purportedly related to my grandfather Maurice's ambitions in the pro-Zionist movement. Her father stayed behind to earn enough money so that the whole family could be together in this new frontier. There, Mom spent an unstable childhood. With her father thousands of miles away, it was left to her to be the constant companion for her own sickly mother. Disastrously, a ruptured appendix left Hannah in the hospital and unwell for months, and young Leah had to board with relatives. To this day, my mother recounts with some bitterness having to live with her distant kin, who were virtual strangers she didn't like, particularly her maternal grandmother whom she later called "that bitch." By the time she had regained some of her health, my grandmother had taken her daughter back to the United States where my grandfather had opened a school for foreign languages in the south part of Philadelphia. Family responsibilities combined with the American economy in shambles had put his pioneering ambitions on hold.

As a child, my mother was bright and ambitious, doing well in school and developing an ardent interest in the piano. The family was poor and, like most families at the height of the Great Depression, got by on very little. As the 1930s wore on and the economy yielded to one of war, the early 1940s saw my mother attending the prestigious Philadelphia High School for Girls where she made high grades and developed into a talented pianist. She then attended Temple University's School of Nursing, became a registered nurse, and moved to New York City where she worked hard, reveled in the cultural scene of recitals, the symphony, and theater, and searched, like a lot of driven young women in those days, for a career and then a husband.

Stepping into that role was my father, Max. He was born in Brooklyn, New York in 1920, the son of an immigrant tailor, Ben, and his wife, Sadie. Like my mother, he was an only child until, again like my mother, a sibling of the opposite sex came along nine years later. Young Max was rebellious, mischievous, stubborn, and clever. There are stories of him getting his head caught between the iron bars of a public railing (the Brooklyn fire department had to liberate him), of disappearing for days at a time at summer camp, and of building rock formations covered in snow and ice to not only block traffic on bridges but to delight in the damage to cars he and his buddies had just unleashed. In later years, Dad would relate how, as a stocky kid in Brooklyn, he would act as sucker-bait for his handball partner. This partner would hustle an opposing twosome and proclaim, "I'll pick any kid from this crowd, and I'll still beat 'cha!" He would always pick my clunky, un-athletic-appearing father, and, together, they would deliberately lose the first game or two only to double the bet and take the dupes for all their money.

In short, Dad was a hell-raiser.

But he was an ambitious hell-raiser. He got his bachelor's in chemistry from NYU and applied to medical school (his own polio-stricken uncle, Izzy, a urologist at the University of Iowa, was his role model) but could not get in due to quotas against admitting Jews. This gave my father an early taste of discrimination firsthand and undoubtedly shaped the way he would see minorities as kindred spirits of sorts. In all the years I knew my dad, his views toward minority groups firmly tended on the side of sympathy.

After college, he earned a master's degree in chemistry at MIT, continued to apply and get rejected to medical school, and wandered to and from chemistry laboratories at locations as diverse as Purdue University in West Lafayette, Indiana to Princeton, New Jersey where, under the Manhattan Project, he had done secret work on the atomic bomb project. After the war, in 1946, he finally gained admission to the Boston University School of Medicine, finished in 1950, and moved to New York City where he did his medical internship and residency. It was there that he met my mother, an operating room nurse at New York City's Mount Sinai Hospital.

My mother had her marital sights set on my father's closest friend, Herman Schwartz, who was eventually my dad's best man at his wedding and was, according to the stories about him, medicine's answer to Cary Grant. Mom actually dated

9

Herman briefly, and once, overjoyed, she overheard him say in the hospital cafeteria that he was going to "marry Leah." Too bad, according to my mother, that it turned out to be a different Leah, the well-known graphic artist, Leah Schwartz, who bagged Herman. Mom would later say that she had to "settle for my father," a pronouncement that made me uncomfortable and wonder if we kids were the offspring of a failed arrangement from the start.

###

Somerset, 1961. Deb, standing; the author with cowboy hat and Lisa, foreground.

Deb, Lisa, and I shared a long rectangular room in Somerset with three single beds in a row against the wall. My bed was closest to the hall door, Lisa's was in the middle near the back porch door, and Deb's was at the end near the window. Three small, alpine-style wooden chairs, one blue, one yellow, and one red, all with straw-lined seat covers, sat in the middle of the room. Three siblings in one room naturally resulted in a bit of a commotion from time to time. One night we three had to bear the brunt of Dad's temper. "If I hear one more peep out of you three," he snarled, "I'll beat you to within an inch of your life! Now, go to sleep, goddamn it!" At which point, just as the door slammed shut, the tiniest utterance of "peep" slipped from Deb's mouth.

In those two and a half years in Somerset, when I was age two to five, memories of my father vacillated from him being hot-tempered and stern to extraordinarily tender. Photos from that time reveal a brawler: stocky, scowling, an unfiltered Camel cigarette dangling from a corner of his mouth, ready to take on anybody who crossed him. His reputation for being both a smart-ass and confrontational was self-admitted and justified.

But Dad's kindness was there, too. Bedridden at age four with mumps and a high fever, I had Dad right by my bedside for what seemed like hours, placing cool compresses on my head and spoon-feeding me Coca-Cola with cracked ice. "Heah, Deah," he'd say in that New York accent, "slowly, slowly ~ that's it...."

On rare summer Saturday evenings toward dusk, Dad could be found on the back porch of the Somerset ranch-style house, reclining in a lounge chair, his pale white legs spread out. There, with a weak bourbon and ginger ale in hand, clinking the ice in the glass the way he used to do, he'd laugh as his three kids played tag and did summersaults near the graceful weeping willow and the smell of freshly cut grass rode with the soft breeze.

About the only time of the week that my dad could get some exercise was Sunday afternoons at Rock Creek Pool. He'd be in the water in his plaid boxer-style bathing suit ~ complete with elastic belt and magnetic metal clasp so popular in the day ~ with my arms around his neck. Staring at his broad, sunburned back, I'd watch as he pinched the snot away, snort with that big Semitic nose of his, and say, "Hang on, Dave! We're goin' under!" as he plunged, walrus-like, into the cool waters. Soon, my two sisters or other kids would be hanging all over him, like remoras on a shark, pleading for the same treatment. "Enough! Let's just have a few at a time," he'd say, three kids clinging to him as he bobbed in the water. "Up and down we go-go-go," he chanted, "and - a up and down we go!" Happy, secure thoughts swirled in my young brain as I anticipated the Sunday evening ritual of a warm shower at home then off to the Hot Shoppes for dinner where we kids would flip the paper place mats over and draw with pencils and crayons until our meals came.

After the workweek had made its rude reappearance, it would be back to Mad Max. As the runt of three kids, I had a notoriously poor appetite and was repulsed by the steak and potatoes dipped in ketchup that my father seemed to live on. "Goddamn it!" he'd say to me, pounding his fist on the kitchen table, making the knives, forks, and spoons dance with the impact. "Eat something!" My habit of spitting out whatever I was forced to eat left me, my mother, and sisters disgusted and further fueled my father's anger. (Luckily, I had King as an capable garbage disposal by my side.) It came to the point where all I could tolerate were hot dogs and peanut butter sandwiches.

Since he was so busy with his growing medical practice, Dad did not have much of a presence around the house. This meant I spent much of my time surrounded by females: Mom, Louise, Deb and Lisa. Somerset showed Mom at her best: creative, slim, athletic, musical ~ always off to a modern dance

Louise towers above the neighborhood kids in Somerset, 1960. The author is at front right.

class, arranging a chamber music soirée for the house, and generally displaying her affectionate and light-hearted side.

Happily, there appeared to be little if any conflict between Mom and Louise. When my older sisters were in school and Mom and I were out doing errands, Louise was left in relative peace. With no savings, no spouse, and her one child, Chester, being cared for in distant part of town and another son, Christopher (the existence of whom, incredibly, I was only made aware by Chester in 2012) put up for adoption, it was in Somerset that Louise finally found herself after many years of wandering.

Louise was thirty-eight years old in 1960. Her parents, Cherry and Thomas Johnson, raised seven girls and three boys. Where Louise fell in order of birth I only learned toward the end of her life. She earned special favor with her father who nicknamed her "Jew" allegedly due to her industriousness and desire for advancement. I have no idea how many Jews lived in her birthplace of Macon at the time, but I know now that it was not unusual in many southern cities of varying sizes in the 1920s South that Jews were heavily represented as merchants. "Them Jews love the pennies," Louise would later tell me, mocking with particular relish her rendition of what she considered was their characteristic accent: "That will be one nyunty-nyun and two fawty-nyun."

Louise was not lucky enough to get much of a "higher" education, though she did graduate high school. She told me amusing and even mystical stories of bricks flying from virtually thin air against the side of an abandoned warehouse and of the workman she spied from the rafters of a barn who had his way with the rear end of a cow. She loved telling that story. " 'Ooooooh-wee!' he cried, 'If you was a woman, I'd buy you a new pair of shoes!' " She'd frequently make reference to a favorite ditty that made rounds at her elementary school in Macon, leaving me squealing with laughter. It involved her teacher, a Miss Dixon:

Miss Dish-rag jumped up and fahrted,
And thas' how it started!

Childhood for Louise meant hard labor, which made for strong arms and legs. She was muscular in a long and lean way. She was tall, about five-ten, and she was solid but not overweight. Her features were beautiful to me: dark eyes; a broad, symmetric nose, teeth like piano keys, cheekbones that reached the sky and silky, ebony skin. She wasn't chesty but not flat either. She kept her hair wavy and short and used long aluminum clips to keep it tidy. Her smile was a million watts of sunshine. Around the house, she wore a sky blue housedress with white trim and white soft-soled shoes along with the ever-present pale blue apron with white lace trim.

Louise had married young and twice. The first time was to a much older man, Felix Holloman, of whom she said little. That marriage lasted but three years. After her next marriage to her second husband, Willie Morris, the couple left Georgia and moved to Mineral Wells, Texas looking for work. (Her son, Chester, later told me that the move was due to Willie's job, something to do with construction, but Louise was never clear on that.) In Texas, Louise had her son, Chester, or "Pete", as she called him. He supposedly shared my birthday, July 29th (although later research by me indicated that he was born on July 28th), and Louise loved to remind me that we boys were alike because we were born "under the same sign of the microscope."

It was not long until she divorced again due to Willie's apparent infidelity ("ho-hoppin'," she called it), and she was forced to support Chester on her own. After a short stint in the kitchen at a country club in North Carolina and moves to Philadelphia, Baltimore, and back to Georgia, she decided to settle in Washington. Why Washington? It was likely due to the fact that her sister, Mary McDade, lived there, having moved down from her last known address in Philadelphia. I never learned what brought Mary to DC.

But Louise's settling on Washington as a place to plan a future was fortuitous for me, and it wasn't long before our lives in the suburbs became further entwined.

Chapter Three

House of Pain

ଛଠଓଔ

Bethesda, Maryland
1962-1965

In August of 1962, when my parents' lease was up on the house in Somerset, we moved to a subdivision in Bethesda called Lybrook. Needing a larger house to accommodate the arrival of my brother, Daniel, Max and Leah bought a home for the princely sum of forty thousand dollars in the subsection of Lybrook artfully named Weathervane Hill. This newer neighborhood, not nearly as stately or established as Somerset, was set between older Woodhaven and Burning Trees Estates, home of the famous Burning Tree Country Club, noteworthy as the playground of presidents and senators (no women allowed.) I turned five that year and attended kindergarten at Burning Tree Elementary, a wondrous place that would play such an important part in my young years. (So special was B.T.E.S. that I can recite all of my teachers' names, in order, to this day to my astounded wife and regale her with dozens of stories that constitute the mythology of Burning Tree. I am still in contact with many of my classmates.)

I had the afternoon shift for that first year of school, and the sixtyish Mrs. Edwards, with her red horn-rimmed glasses, pearls, heavy lipstick, and pale complexion, presided over finger-painting, songs, the alphabet, and the playground. Early on, I learned something about my penchant for nostalgia and longing (early harbingers of my later depressions), which showed itself in strange behaviors. I learned that the way I oriented my body and eyes, even the direction I was facing, had a profound effect on my mood. A primitive, developing,

Fun on West Howell Road, 1966. Top, left to right: Belle Broad, grandmother Hannah Lipschutz, my mother Leah and Louise. Foreground: Michael Collins, the author, Kenny Langille and Bobby Burgerman.

kindergarten "feng shui" was taking hold of me, lurking inside and fighting to get out. Exploring the Burning Tree Elementary playground that first autumn, I would climb a wrought-iron-framed rocket ship, so early-1960s in its design. Blistering hot in early fall and cold to the touch in winter, it made the perfect perch to orient my gaze toward my home, a mere two miles away, and long for where my security and comfort lay.

Those were the times, so similar to the days in Somerset, when Mom and Weezy got along almost like sisters. They used to dance in the kitchen, Louise with her blue uniform and apron, and my mother, slender and tanned from the summer sun, in a skirt and blouse. Seeing Louise and my mother this way filled me with gladness and ease. Juking side by side, they could have been two twirling salt and pepper shakers. Hurtling down the stairs to go out and play, I would catch a glimpse of Mom and Weezy in the hall bathroom, Louise's fingers covered in hair dye and buried deep in my mother's scalp, the two of them trading small talk as the brown liquid ran down the sides of the plastic sheeting around my mom's neck like chocolate syrup on a sundae.

Like many Jews of the 1960s, my mother was rather liberal in her politics. As a teenager, she attended Zionist and left-leaning summer camps in rural Massachusetts and Pennsylvania. Largely, American Jews had the deserved reputation of favoring Democrats over Republicans, and my parents were no exception. While never really active in politics (I cannot recall them ever making any special effort to get to the polls on Election Day), they always supported the donkey's candidate: Johnson, Humphrey, McGovern for sure. This leftward-leaning meant that civil rights were valued, fostered by the fact that at least 30 to 40 percent of my father's patients were black or minorities. Many of these people could not afford to pay fully, or at all, for his services, so my dad ate a lot of the cost. As a result, his back office was papered with appreciative notes from many who expressed gratitude for the cut-rate yet quality care they received. I used to love reading them.

That's not to say that my parents did not hold some prevailing unflattering views of blacks and other minorities. In many Jewish households, blacks were called "schvartzes," which, literally, means "blacks." The derogatory nature of this, in linguistic circles at least, is still debated. Much to my embarrassment, my mother, like many of her friends, referred to the poorer, blacker sections of DC as "Deepest, Darkest Africa." But I took comfort in the many times my mother would tell me that Philadelphia High School for Girls had many black students in her day and that she was proud of that.

The family dynamic changed in Bethesda as Weezy spent more time with the three older children (Deborah, nine; Lisa, seven; and me, five) and Mom tended to her new baby, Daniel. My father was working long hours and not coming home until late. Then bad things started to happen. In late summer of 1962, Lisa started losing weight. She was thirsty all the time and urinated frequently. It didn't take long for my endocrinologist father to diagnose her with diabetes, the disease that would eventually kill her at age twenty-seven.

Now my mother had to deal with a new baby, whom she later claimed was unplanned, and an even sicker child. My eldest sister, Deb, was exerting her preteen independence, and my father was having problems in his practice with an inflexible and overbearing partner. The end result was that I ended up spending more time alone with Louise, and she gradually replaced my mother as nurturer and caregiver.

Weathervane Hill differed from Somerset as the homes tended to be larger, there were more children to play with, and there was more room to run around and explore. New construction was everywhere, and there was no shortage of ways to get dirty. Our street ended in a cul-de-sac beneath which ran Booze Creek, a tributary of the Cabin John watershed in lower Montgomery County, Maryland. The algae and mud as well as the dirt and clay unearthed from new construction afforded me ample opportunity to get both filthy and wet, and it fell on Louise to hose me down. She gave me baths, and when another kid monopolized the tub, I received one of her vigorous "wipe-offs" with soap and a scratchy washcloth. A typical clean-up went like this:

Weezy: "C'mon, Davis. Les' get you clean. You looks and smells like a country pig!" (She started calling me "Davis" because her comment around the house was "Dave-is my favorite boy! I knows him when I sees him!")

Then she'd sing to me:

"Red, white, and blue, stars over you!

Red, white, and pank — you sho' do stank!"

By the time I was seven, Louise started calling me made-up pet names like "turkey bird" and "old man" and informed me that I was too big for her to pick up any longer. Whenever I appeared sad or out of sorts, she'd sing me this nonsense song to the tune of "Ten Little Indians:"

You be well, 'fo you marry
You be well, 'fo you marry
You be well, 'fo you marry
Jump up, little boy! You ain't hurt no way!

I loved to watch her from my perch on the refrigerator,
Lord of the Kitchen Kingdom. From there, I looked on in
wonder as she prepared dinner, which was heavy on Crisco
and foods I wasn't familiar with. She would pick poke
"salit" from the backyard and make sassafras tea. Her fried
potatoes filled the room with an earthy aroma, and the
fried chicken snapped and hissed in the skillet. My father,
half-jokingly, complained that she was trying to kill him
with her cooking.

With a new baby in the house and a chronically ill
daughter, my parents' relationship started to show signs of
fatigue. Mom was tied up with Lisa, getting her to doctors'
appointments, audiologists, and psychologists. Deb was in
her own world of horses, the Beatles, pencil-drawing, and
rebelling against my parents. Dad was gaining weight, tired
of work and straining under the growing suburban stress.
Daniel was just a toddler. Me? I had my school, my friends,
my increasing talent for sports, and, most of all, Louise.
Louise? She had work. "It's good for the mind," she'd say.

Mom had a nascent but quickly maturing habit of
envying the lifestyle of other doctors' wives, some of whom
lived in the neighborhood. What kindled a change in my
mother's attitude regarding her social standing may have
ignited with a simple social ritual. To break the tensions of
the week, my parents would venture out on Saturday nights
to join other doctors and their wives for dinner, drinks, and
dancing. They all belonged to a medical fraternity, Phi Delta

Epsilon, which was made up of Jewish couples from similar socio-economic backgrounds.

I can remember being alone with Weezy and Daniel in the house on such nights while my older sisters were out with friends. My brother and I, along with our black and tan dachshund, Freddie, shared the uppermost room. (Freddie, from a line of champions, née "Graf Bruno von Sregor" by his breeders, was renamed by Deb as Freddie and given the name "Mr. Lickey" by Louise because of his ever-eager tongue. Louise used to say to him: "Freeeee-die; come get ya'lls meeeeeea-ty!" "Look, Davis," she'd say, "hear how his foots go 'cacka-cacka'" on the slate floor. Dad dubbed him "The Knight of the Darting Tongue.")

Whenever my mother would return from a night out with the Phi D E gang, she'd come to kiss Danny and me goodnight reeking of perfume, cigarettes, and alcohol. Then it was off to her bedroom where, after the TV was on and a half hour or so had passed, the fighting with my father would begin. I could hear the muffled voices behind closed doors, punctuated by sharp recriminations and shouts. A typical exchange sound like this:

"Why are you always putting me down in front of other people?" Mom would yell. "You really are a bastard, you know. I guess it makes you feel like a big man!"

"Oh, Leah. Why don't you just go to hell! I'm tired of listening to your bullshit. Your problem is you have it too good!"

"Too good?! Who has it too good? I don't understand a doctor who sleeps so late and plays golf three days a week. How are you going to build a practice like that? Your problem is you don't like yourself! If you did, you'd be more successful, like Bob!"

"Oh, go fuck yourself!"

Never totally sure of what they were fighting over, I would inevitably hear my mother leave the room, slam the bedroom door, and head downstairs to the "Gorgeous," the name my brother gave to the recently redecorated living room. On the velvet crimson couch in the sea of green shag carpet, my mother would cry, and I would have to make the usual descent to comfort her. Wiping away tears, she would tell me there was nothing I could do to help her. It made me feel awful and powerless.

If the fighting got white-hot, Mom would storm out of the house, the door slamming and its brass knocker clunking heavily behind, and tear up the street in the station wagon. I was terrified, pressing my nose against the pane in my bedroom window, my rapid breaths fogging and defogging the glass, watching and hearing as the car's engine noise and taillights faded over the crest of West Howell Road. Not knowing when or if she would come back, I stayed awake until all hours when she would return from the Biograph movie theater in downtown DC after sublimating her sorrows in some 60s flick.

Fighting. Fighting. Seemingly endless fighting. T. Rex versus Triceratops. Ali versus Frazier. It never stopped. It was not confined to the privacy of the home, however. The general public had to share in the festivities. On the way to Brooklyn to see my father's parents, Dad would drive the old Pontiac station wagon and Mom would be in the front. Lisa and Deb would occupy the back seat (without seat belts, of course, as was the custom of the day), and I would be in the "way-back" like some Middle Eastern emir, covered in pillows, blankets, comforters, and stuffed toys. I'd lie down, head to the rear, facing up and watching as the street and highway lights we passed rapidly descended their reflections on the inside surface of the back window. This gave the exciting illusion of ascending in a space ship and kept me rapt for hours on the trip.

Once we had crossed the Verrazano Bridge into Brooklyn, my reverie would be interrupted:

"Max, you sure you know the directions? This is where we always get lost!"

"Shut up, Leah. I know where I'm going. We've done this a hundred times."

"Watch out! There's a lady who wants to get by in that red car!"

"I can see, Leah. I'm not blind. Huh (muttering)...what does she think SHE's doing? Cut me off, will ya? (He rolls down the window and yells to the driver.) 'What the hell do you think you're doin'? Can't you see I was here first?' "

"Max! Just leave it alone!"

"Shut up, Leah! (Readdressing the driver) 'Oh, yeah, lady. Well, same to you! You can just go SUCK!' "

In restaurants, it was no different:

David: "Can I get a Coke, Dad?"

Max: "Sure you can get a Coke."

Leah: "But only one. It'll spoil your dinner. Besides, we have to set limits."

Max: "Oh, leave the kid alone."

Leah: "You see? You're always too permissive with them. We have to present a united front! (Exasperated.) Now, one Coke, and that's it!"

Lisa: "How come David gets a Coke? I want a Coke."

Mom: "Lisa, you know you're not allowed Coke."

Lisa cries.

Max: "Now look what you've started, Leah!"

By this time, the noise and tension would have attracted the attention of other diners. My mother, her face flushed with rage, would dip her hand in her water glass and flick water into my father's face, saying, "Howdya' like that, big shot?"

I would bury my head under the table. My stomach would start to hurt, and I'd want to leave.

Experiences like that taught me bitter lessons early on. The crimes that parents commit against their children ~ crimes that often get perpetrated on succeeding generations ~ often go unnoticed and more certainly unpunished. And yet it is the child's chemistry that will often dictate the psychological outcome. In the 1960s, as today, the crimes against children were not restricted to parents. In fact, despite my parents' increasingly apparent dysfunctional relationship, pockets of clueless adults seemed to be everywhere.

One example: in early grade school, a lot of my friends were joining the Cub Scouts, and my parents brought to my attention that perhaps I should consider it as well. After attending the orientation meeting with my mother, she bought the uniform, got me the written propaganda, and off I went to study for the Big Pledge Night. I had to memorize the Boy Scout Pledge; you know, the one that goes, "On my honor, I will do my best, to do my duty, to God and my country..." Blah blah blah.

There I am with Mom on Pledge Night. When my turn came to get up in front of everyone, I was appropriately nervous. Standing straight as I could with three fingers of my right hand cocked next to my ear, I recited what I thought to be a flawless rendition of The Pledge. I gave a sigh of relief and glanced over to my mother who gave me a nod. "Glad that's done with," I thought. Not so fast. Before my butt hit the seat, the scoutmaster turned to all and said, "Who can tell me what young David did wrong?" Incredulous, I looked at him with a mixture of embarrassment and wonder. The room fell silent. "David failed to raise his hand high to the sky," the asshole said. "Since we are all proud scouts," he went on, "we need to raise our hands high when we recite The Pledge." That's all I needed to hear. At least I had the self-knowledge and respect to know that I wanted no part of an organization whose first official act was to publicly humiliate me. That was the last day I had anything to do with the Cub Scouts.

Other crimes were committed. As early as second grade, it had been planted into my head that I would become a doctor. (I've heard it said in Jewish philosophy that the time when a fetus becomes a human being is when it graduates medical school.) My mother would remark nonchalantly, "You don't want to be a doctor? No? That's fine." This would be followed by a drop of the head and downcast eyes. "You could always sell shoes...." She'd further reinforce this "doctor" drumbeat by using my brother as a prop: "Danny, are you hurt? Go see Doctor David; he'll make it all better."

My father's bedroom was stacked and riddled with hundreds of old and then current medical journals. (I was afraid to touch some of the hideous pictures in those pages for fear that some exotic and dreadful disease might rub off on my fingers.) He also brought home promotional knickknacks from drug companies ~ plastic hearts, kidneys, and even hands that you could open up and peer at the inner workings. I can remember feeling a sense of specialness, a rarified self-importance because I came from a "medical family." People relied on me, I convinced myself, for my superior judgment and insight into the human body.

In the coatroom one day at Burning Tree, the kids discovered a trail of red drops on the floor. In actuality it was the disgusting ketchup someone had brought back from the school cafeteria in one of those small, frilly paper cups. Like some modern-day mixture of Galen and Sherlock Holmes, I knelt on one knee next to the evidence and weighed in on whether this was indeed ketchup or, more ominously, blood from some poor student or faculty member. Gravely (and erroneously), I pronounced it to be blood, and, remarking that this was a "very serious matter," stated that we must begin the search for the injured party so that aid could be given right away. (Dad's use of ketchup and memories of my responsibilities at Burning Tree have resulted in my lifelong ketchup phobia, a source of much amusement to my wife and son.)

Apparent to me now, hints of mild but increasing emotional pathology were sprouting their tendrils that year in second grade. One was my growing OCD. I used to love to draw birds, and I would pride myself in what I thought to be pretty decent renditions on the huge sheaves of Manila paper that lived in the art supply closet in the back of the room. If I felt I had made the slightest mistake, however, instead of merely erasing the flaw, I would rip the whole thing up and begin anew lest someone might discover my huge talents and want to place that particular work in the Smithsonian or the Louvre. The self-described masterpieces of robins, jays, and crows that met my exacting standards were signed "David Sh.," not "David S.," lest they be confused with another "David" in my class.

One day, I noticed that on one of my graceful creations my signature had been altered. To the "Sh" I had carefully placed after "David" the letters "it" had been added. The culprit ~ my nemesis and sometime playmate, Brad ~ eventually was proved guilty and punished by the teacher. Again, my specialness was noted and vindicated, I thought.

If the "nurture" aspect of my early childhood had its shortcomings, at least the "nature" part afforded me some advantages. It is fair to say that I come from a family of people with an ear for language and music. My mother's father ran his own preparatory school in Philadelphia, and he was multilingual. So too with my mother's brother, my mother, my brother and sister, and myself. My mother and brother are also talented pianists, and I, too, studied the piano in college. In fact, it was my major. As a child, I had a keen ear for language and mimicry. On the rare occasions when they got along, my parents got a taste of my skits, imitations, and parodies at the foot of their bed.

With all the time I had to spend alone with Louise, I was fortunate to soak up her dialect, accent, and phrases, and it is no surprise to me that, if there is such a thing, my black American English is the best of any white man's in these United States. (Even in 2013, my mother, sister, brother, and I still lapse into this same patois when the mood strikes us.)

Luckily for me, Louise's word choices, syntax, and pronunciation enriched my life in ways I never could have imagined. On the most basic level, everyone in the family got a new name. Daniel became "Danyu" or "Danyun," Lisa became "Pizza," I became "Davis," and my mother, Leah, was simply "yo' momma" or, formally, "Miss Sheer." Even King, our dog, became "Kang." I can still hear her sing, to the tune of the theme song of the old TV show, *Wyatt Earp*:

"Kangy-poo, I love you. Brave, courageous and bold!"

Gradually, I became aware of Louise's expressions -- so rich and colorful as to make a huge impression on an eight-year-old boy with an ear and brain for music and language. She warned me that if I didn't learn to defend myself, some boys would "beat the starch" out of me. Some friends of my parents were perceived as being so wealthy as to "have enough money to cremate a wet mule" or be "rich as cream." People who sported wrinkles were "broke in the face," and those who had freckles were "speckle-faced." Constipation was expressed as "havin' the locked bowels." When Mom started to increasingly lose her temper, Louise said Mom would "raise sand" (raise Satan?). "I ain't stutin' about you" was clearly a bastardization of "studying about you" made apparent to me in a later reading of the work of Flannery O'Connor in her masterpiece of Southern Gothic, *The Violent Bear It Away*. And if people appeared to be ignorant they wouldn't know "they goddamn asshole from a shotgun." "Yo's gotcha own shorts on, ain't cha'?" meant "mind your own business," and looking "squintch-eyed" at someone was to regard them with suspicion. If food "slipped down the wrong throat" that meant it was blocking your windpipe instead of heading to your stomach. My balled-up fist was my "soup-bone," and whenever I did something that pleased Louise or made her proud, she'd ask me to let her kiss my fist - a way of giving her my "soup-bony to chew own-y." Casual clothing was merely "round home clothes." And to "favor" someone meant that you bore a resemblance to him or her. Indeed, years later, the pretty girl who lived across the street gave me this remembrance of Louise: "You favor your momma so much it's like she done throwed you up."

As my elementary school years progressed, I found myself speaking and even thinking in two distinct languages: American English and Louise English. This language link that Louise and I held only increased my affection for her. Often upon hearing one her legendary malapropisms, I was compelled to throw my arms around her waist out of sheer love and joy, planting my face in her stomach and taking in her complex bouquet. She reliably smelled of Ivory soap and Noxema, which she used to keep her beautiful skin so soft. I came to love her so much that I would squeal like a piglet: "Wee wee wee" (short for Weezy), a hug-squeeze punctuating each exclamation. My anchor, my rock, my protector, she would literally have my back if I broke wind, explaining: "Child, they's mo' room on the outside than on the inside!"

Not only did I learn Louise's distinctive dialect, but she helped me discover things no city boy would know. Having been brought up on a farm, her extensive knowledge of animals and their ways taught me a bitter lesson. Dad had purchased some duck chicks for me, the motivation of which escapes me, and Louise warned me not to allow large amounts of food to remain in their basement pen. Thinking that idea was ridiculous and that they would stop eating when full, I was shocked to return later to find them all stone-cold dead, having been literally split open by eating uncontrollably. "Now, Davis," Louise reprimanded me gently. "I done told you not to do that. It's in they genes and they chromiums, don't you see? They can't hep it!"

In fact, all of us kids should have heeded Louise's knowledge of animal husbandry for our growing menagerie suffered under our careless watch. There was Horatio, the one-legged parakeet, rendered disabled when Lisa carelessly took off a lower extremity while trimming his tail feathers with a scissor. Daniel's grouper, Oscar, barely able to move in his too-small aquarium, was covered in the fish disease "ick." A variety of guinea pigs, hamsters, and turtles were all in varying states of health, and a horned toad squirted blood from his eyes. All these poor creatures had their lives cut down too short by the Grim Pet Reaper. Only the cats and dogs seemed to flourish.

By my middle childhood, life at home grew more complicated as my parents' relationship became even more strained. Fights between them became increasingly loud and frequent, and their nighttime arguments disrupted my sleep. A seminal event in the lore of the Sherer household occurred when my mother claimed that her back was permanently injured when Daniel ran out into the street from our parked car, her entreaties to my father to run after him falling on deaf ears. I was there, but it all happened so quickly that what is true memory and what is not is difficult to say. My mother recalls yelling, "Max! Quick! Danny's running into the street! Get him!" and my father responding, "Go pick him up yourself, ya fuckin' bitch." Wherever the truth lies, Mom did pick him up, "slipped some discs," and spent more than half a lifetime blaming my father for her chronic back problems. Given my father's temper and less than stellar relationship with his wife, I tend to support my mother's version of events.

After her back injury, my mom's already faltering parenting skills headed further south. Childhood visits to the pediatrician were never pleasant for me, and invariably my first question to my mother was "Am I going to get a shot?" The answer was always the same: "I DON'T know!" spoken with the same irritated inflection each time. My pediatrician, Dr. Coleman, was a pock-faced, middle-aged man who always instructed me to undress by saying only,

"Peel." Whenever I came to his office dirty or smelly from playing, he would call it "boy dirt." The dread of every visit was whether I was going to get those miserable tuberculin tine tests ~ the ones that have the four prongs like an old-fashioned phone jack ~ or whether I'd receive the sinister-sounding tetanus "booster" shot, the one that hurt bad at the beginning and even worse the next few days.

On one occasion while waiting for the pediatrician, I was afflicted with what most boys about that age suffer at one time or another: the random erection. I can remember how things went down (or up) in those childhood days. Even the mere jiggling of the bus would cause my penis to swell. At that time, the only way to effectively cover up such an embarrassment was to get off the bus and use textbooks to cover up front what was going on behind. While waiting in the pediatrician's office with my mother, I had a huge boner lurking under my corduroys. My mother's gaze drifted down to my nether parts. Without warning or much expression on her face, she took her two fingers and unceremoniously poked on the front of my pants, remarking, "Oh! An erection... I guess you're old enough to get those by now!" I was mortified. And as any man knows, the best way to sink an erection (which I so desperately needed to do before the nurse or old Doc Coleman came in) is to think of something depressing. Death, Famine, Plague, Pestilence ~ any one of the Four Horseman would do. But this sucker wouldn't deflate until the very last second, just as pock-marked Coleman came in and told me to "peel."

Admittedly, my mother's indelicate parenting and the intermittent intrusions of my own burgeoning sexuality were the least of my family's problems. Lisa's health continued to worsen, and there were other issues. Deb had been hit in the head by a golf club by a neighbor at a driving range and suffered a depressed skull fracture. An inch lower would have cost her left eye, and she required forty-five stitches to close the wound. Three-year-old Daniel accidentally mistook a full bottle of Lomotil anti-diarrheal pills for candy one summer afternoon and ended up at Children's National Hospital just as my parents and I were returning from picking Lisa up at Camp NYDA for diabetic children in New York state. It was Louise who literally saved Daniel's life, running across the street to Dr. Burgerman who alerted the ambulance and took charge of the situation. "Dr. Boigerman!" she recounted later as saying, "call the rescue squaw so they can take me and this baby in an avalanche to the hospital!" Tragedy seemed to be all around, and I came to depend more and more on Louise for love and support.

Most assuredly, Norman Rockwell would not have chosen to paint this family, and the most glaringly missing subject on that illustrator's absent canvas would have been its matriarch. The happy, creative mother I knew in Somerset had become a different person in Bethesda. Envious of other doctors' wives and their lifestyles, she berated my father because, in her view, he didn't work enough or because we didn't belong to country clubs or drive fancy cars. Louise's take on the situation was: "Them Jewish womens loves to fuss!"

By 1965, my eighth year, my mother, in my father's view, was well on her way to becoming the quintessential Jewish wife. On a late fall afternoon while watching a commercial during a Redskins game in the den, my father drew a big puff from his Hoyo de Monterrey cigar, set it gingerly in the green-glass ashtray, turned to me, and related the old joke: "What's the difference between a vulture and a Jewish mother? The vulture tears your heart out only after it kills you..." It was a species of humor that my young ears could not quite comprehend.

Looking back, I can only guess at what happened to my mother. This lies, I believe, in our "genes and chromiums." My mother comes from a line of depressed and anxious people. Her mother was certainly that way, and, to my misfortune, I later concluded that many of my ancestors, with varying degrees of intensity and penetrance, shared some expression of the illness. My father was certainly depressed, but that could have been more situational that endogenous. A good physician friend has this theory: In Jews, anxiety and the resultant depression are somehow adaptive and selective in perpetuating the culture. Because of persecution, it was the Jew who, constantly looking over his or her own shoulder, anticipating trouble and wary of "what might happen," was able to survive and produce the next generation. Whether there is a shred of truth in this or not, I leave to the researchers and social scientists.

I struggled to understand why I deserved a family where the stars misaligned to such an extent. Disease and mayhem seemed to be laying fingers on family members, one by one. Disastrously and cruelly, my father was insidiously developing trigeminal neuralgia, or tic douloureux, a painful facial nerve condition that the medical textbooks characterize as so severe it causes many a sufferer to commit suicide.

Trigeminal neuralgia, like childbirth and passing a kidney stone, is one of the most painful conditions any human can endure. In the middle 1960s, my father began experiencing right-side facial pain, burning and stabbing in character. As is typical with this disease, he made many doctor and dentist visits and, after many pulled teeth and misdiagnoses, finally found a neurologist who made the correct call. Before the 1960s, there was no good treatment for the disease (short of a bullet to the head) as pharmaceuticals had not come along and surgical procedures were not perfected. Many of the sufferers sank into depression, weight loss, withdrawal, drug abuse, and utter despair.

There was a Swedish diplomat living on our block who had access to drugs from Europe not available at that time in the United States. My father had heard about a new drug, Tegretol, that he was excited to try. Before pharmaceuticals were available, my father had started to drink alcohol to dull the pain. My father was never much of a drinker, but this was the only thing that helped him ease the pain for some of the time. I could always tell when he was suffering from a bout of "tic" because he would start to alter his speech. The best way I can describe it is "stiff" with very little lip movement. He also grew a mustache because he couldn't shave over the area that was painful. Cold weather and wind were excruciating, which he described as multiple knives stabbing him in the face. After starting Tegretol, he was able to titrate the dose to the amount that would give him the most relief without sedating him too much.

I made a careful study of my father's disease, as did he. Oddly, food would give him some relief, and it would take about five or ten minutes after ingesting for his pain level to go down anywhere between 50 and 80 percent. He was also highly affected by stress. Whenever there was work-related or family strife, his pain increased to the level where I could tell something was going on. He started to speak hesitantly. He didn't want to do anything but lie down in the den anesthetized by the television. He retreated away from his often humorous and extroverted personality.

Tegretol, like golf, was a godsend for my father. It made life bearable as it afforded at least partial respite.

For the rest of the family, respite was scarce. My sister, Lisa, and my parents were faced with the very bleak reality of dealing with juvenile diabetes. My mother was contending with increasing back pain and anger and resentment at my father's perceived shortcomings. Deb, whose pharmaceutical proclivities gelled with the prevailing times, was trying to escape the madness, and Daniel was merely a three year old. That left me clinging to Louise, my life preserver in twelve-foot seas.

Like a survivor after a bus bombing in an Israeli bus station, eardrums blown out and legs splayed every which angle on the ground, I was left wondering what the hell had happened after the explosion occurred and the metal scraps and body parts had hit the street and windows. Since moving from Somerset to Bethesda, all the disasters ~ Lisa's illness, Deb's serious golf club injury, Daniel's near-death overdose, my father's facial pain, my mother's back malady and her disappointment about her place in the Jewish doctors' wives mini-universe of Bethesda, Maryland of 1965 ~ had left me bewildered and exhausted. I felt like the last man-child standing.

Writing forty-six years later, I've come to understand why Louise was so crucial to my personality development and sense of security. She represented everything that my parents were not: a voice of reason, the classic underdog, a downtrodden yet smiling, warm, and affectionate presence in the midst of chaos. The more my parents fought, especially at night, the more I felt the sting of the tragedies thrown their way and the more I depended on Louise for comfort and stability. I can still hear my dad, as he watched me wrap my arms around her beautiful black neck, say, "David loves his Weezy."

Chapter Four

House on Fire

ℰℭ

Bethesda, Maryland

1965-1969

In the summer of 1965, my parents insisted that I go away to summer camp at Camp Airy in Thurmont, Maryland, not far from Camp David, the retreat of presidents. Camp Airy was an all-boys Jewish camp that drew from families in DC and Baltimore. My sisters went, appropriately, to Camp Louise, the sister camp. How homesick, insecure, and miserable I was at that place! Each summer, I begged my parents not to send me, but they forced me to go. I was probably one of the world's most depressed, unhappy campers.

When not being tormented by the obnoxious kids from Baltimore, forced to swim naked in the frigid outdoor pool at 7:00 a.m. (what was THAT all about?), or eat the disgusting kosher food and drink the sickly sweet "bug juice," we had daily inspection of the bunks. Each morning, the hairy, fat, sarcastic, balding bunk inspector paraded up and down, grading our bed-making skills, the neatness of our cubbyholes, and the tautness of hospital corners of the sheets. He would exult in saying, "I wanna be able to bounce a quarter off these sheets!" "Prick!" I thought. To me, I was like Gomer Pyle, USMC, with Sgt. Carter screaming orders on the hapless private. I hated that goddamn place.

Summers spent at home were a different story entirely. I had my bike, my friends, the labyrinthine construction projects around the neighborhood to play in, my dog Freddie, the neighbors' pool, friends up the street to play "Army guys" and build model cars with, and, of course, Louise. Dad was working all the time. Mom was off with Lisa or Daniel, and Deb was anywhere but home.

One summer, my misery at camp was so bad that I was able to convince my parents to take me home early. If my home life was so full of strife, why did I yearn to return? The answer has to be fear. Fear that my parents, whose tempers could melt tungsten, would divorce. Fear that Louise, as a result, would disappear. Fear that the whole stinkin' house of cards would come crashing down, leaving you know who, the firstborn male of an upwardly mobile Eastern Conservative Jewish Household, to pick up the pieces.

What really kept me going in those days, at seven, eight, and nine years old? What made me happy, secure, amused? A dozen kids to go wild with in our beautiful hilly, wooded neighborhood. An abundance of nature. Trees. Creeks. Mud. Hills. Earth-movers and back hoes. A bike. And, of course, all the wondrous trappings of the mid 1960s: Coke machines where you liberated the 8 ounce bottle from the metal prongs; Nehi Orange and Nehi Grape; the Good Humor Man with his Nutty Buddy, Chocolate Éclairs, and

Toasted Almond; skates with skate keys to tighten them; Popsicle sticks (sharpened on the curb into little daggers until your knuckles bled); the Sinclair dinosaur blow-up beach toy; my suction cup arrow and bow; my Daisy air rifle; Bugs Bunny; baseball cards; Beany and Cecil; Popeye; Tonka toys; model cars and ships and planes you built yourself with airplane glue; footie pajamas; the way-back of the station wagon; a new radium painted glow-in-the-dark watch from E.J. Korvette's; sledding down steep West Howell Road with boots hooked into the open space of the Flexible Flyer behind you; comic books; Mr. Bubble; Sweet Tarts; Pixy Stix; pet turtles with terrariums; the smell of a new football jersey; oiling my baseball glove; and my first set of Wilson boy's golf clubs complete with wooden driver, a 3, 5, 7, and 9 iron, sand wedge putter, and bag. And, oh, the glove that came with it.

Stubbornly, my parents stayed together "for the children" (the tragedy of which we three remaining offspring still discuss today), and the family remained intact. Weezy's place in the household was, at least temporarily, secure. To my continuing comfort, her schedule by that time had become firmly established. Her days off were Thursday evening and all of Sunday. That meant, since she didn't drive (she'd never be able to afford a car, anyway) my mother or father would have to take her to the bus stop at Friendship Heights, or "the District Line." I'd often insist on coming along on the twenty-minute trip to see her off. She would get dressed up in her best clothes, hair done up so slick and nice and chocolate skin so smooth and fresh. She would wear some lipstick. She'd carry a suitcase with her, and there was a hint of perfume in the air. I knew these were the only times she had to visit her son, Chester, who was Deb's age, and it struck me odd that a mother could see her child for only two days per week.

By her third year living in our closely knit Bethesda neighborhood, Louise had become famous, even legendary. Everyone ~ kids and adults ~ loved looking on as she strolled the street, playing with the kids and animals, her trademark brilliant smile, self-effacing manner, and subtle humor ever evident. She appreciated the graciousness of one of our neighbors, a man both great and genteel. Frederick G. Vosburgh, the late former editor of *National Geographic* magazine, lived with his wife, Pat, on our street. Whenever no one was available to take Louise into DC, she hauled her heavy satchel down to the bus stop three quarters of a mile to Bradley Blvd. where she would catch the bus to Friendship Heights. Mr. and Mrs. Vosburgh would often take their daily stroll about that time and were sure to acknowledge Louise. Louise liked to sum up her feelings of the couple by saying, "I like the Vosboigs, especially him. He always tip his hat."

Whenever I could, I would accompany my father or mother picking up Louise on Thursday and Sunday nights. She'd be deposited off the DC Transit bus, and I'd run up to her with a big hug, smelling her still moth-balled infused clothes. Sitting next to her in the backseat of the station wagon, holding her hand and looking up at that noble profile, I would ask about Chester and what she did on her day off. A lot of times she talked about the Harvest Spiritual Church where she was an elder. She spoke little about Chester or a social life. There was scant talk of men and when there was it was with disdain. I'd once overheard her tell my mother, "They don't care how old or ugly you is, long as you've got a hole in your body."

The details of the arrangement for Chester's care was never clear. Louise told me that a woman named Viola cared for him somewhere in the poorer section of DC ~ and there were plenty of those ~ and I would imagine one of those broken-down brownstones near Capitol Hill I used to see when my dad would take me to Constitution Hall or the Library of Congress to hear concerts or to Union Station to pick up an out-of-towner. I envisioned poor dark figures on a stoop, Chester in some dingy room, skinny and tall, not a little bit hungry, with worn-out clothes.

How close this was to reality I never did learn. In fact, I had only met Chester a handful of times in the twenty-two years I knew Louise. One of those times may have been at our house on a July 29th since we (almost) shared the same birthday. He was tall, and in his teenage years he reached six feet eight inches in height. He resembled Louise in face and body, and his head was shaved and elongated in the crown. One time he even let me rub his scalp, my palm widening over the scratchy surface. It felt like coarse sandpaper, and I marveled at the sensation. I knew nothing of his schooling, likes and dislikes, relationships, anything except that his mother saw him those precious few times a week and he had no father to raise him. He lived in Northeast, DC, the kind of place they would show on the TV in black-and-white during the DC MLK assassination riots. I was a child of the green suburbs.

His lot in life didn't sit well with me. Indeed, by the time I was almost ten, I had established some solidified views about blacks, whites, and the social differences between them ~ views that never would have even occurred to me had Louise not come into my life. To me, it is not hard to figure, given my prevailing views of Louise's character and behavior versus those of my mother that my sympathies, uninformed and inchoate as they may have been, lay with the disadvantaged, the people looked down upon ~ the blacks. And since DC was and is "The Chocolate City," there were plenty of blacks to interact with. (It also didn't hurt that most of my sports heroes ~ Bobby Mitchell, Charley Taylor, Willie Mays, Wilt Chamberlain, Roberto Clemente, Bob Gibson ~ were all black.) According to my mother, I had begun to identify too much with them. Whenever in public places like the street, the bus, in buildings, and shopping centers, I would purposely smile and wave to blacks. This bothered my mother, and she'd say:

"Don't DO that! They think you are making fun of them! They will think you are patronizing them!"

I didn't even know what "patronizing" meant. What I did know was that, more than anyone alive, Louise gave me cause to be happy. She didn't expect anything from me other than my contentment. Yes, she wanted me to "get my lesson," as she called doing my homework, and practice the piano, and be great at sports, and so on, but she governed with a velvet glove, not the iron fist my mom (and sometimes my dad) had wielded. She also aroused in me, most evident to my mother, a seemingly inexplicable and irrational kinship with black people, an attitude that would refine and mature as I got older and more knowledgeable about history, politics, economics, religion, human nature, and all the factors that go into how one group of people views themselves and others. Had I never known Louise or what it was like to grow up with a black person living full-time in our house and so divorced from my own background, I cannot fully predict how different a human I would be.

This I do know: By living with Louise ~ subservient, a minority, a woman who made incredible sacrifices in the face of adversity ~ I eventually learned what no book, school, or seminar could teach. I understood, firsthand, the hardships, challenges, and unjust obstacles the less favored groups in society must endure to "make it" in this life. That, and my father's limitless empathy as a physician (despite a hot temper

At the foot of the Puerto Rican rain forest, El Yunque, December 1965.

and rough edges), taught me that one should see people for not what they are but who they are.

In December 1965, the entire family, including Louise, took a holiday trip to Puerto Rico. By this time, my parents were going at it pretty good and very often. I was eight years old, and it was the first time I had been on a plane. So, too, with Louise. We flew in Eastern Airlines Boeing 707 Starstream Whisperjet to Miami and then on to San Juan. Marveling at the meal trays, I took notice of the tiny, individual salt and pepper shakers, metal utensils, and plastic cups and plates all marked with the Eastern Airline plane-in-profile logo and in their trademark colors of sky blue and aqua. I watched Louise closely during that flight down, knowing we were both flying virgins. I was fascinated with the whole ordeal ~ clouds, G-forces, cars and people appearing like ants on the ground. Turbulence. Louise sat transfixed, eyes straight ahead, squeezing the armrest, and I was not sure what she made of the whole thing. Being smart but unschooled, she marveled how this massive metal tube with a wing pinned to each side, full of chattering humans, pre-packaged food, drink, and pinging lights, could transport a group of strangers thousands of miles to a world so different from anything she had ever seen area in DC. The trees were tropical, the mountains imposing, the people dressed differently, and everyone ~ black, white, and every hue in between ~ spoke the same strange language.

Christmas is celebrated, I discovered, differently in Puerto Rico than on the mainland. Yes, there was Christmas on December 25th, but there was The Festival of the Three

Kings, as well. Never having seen this celebrated in the United States, I was puzzled one evening, standing alone on the porch of the rented house in Luquillo Beach, as a procession came down the street more suited to Mardi Gras in New Orleans than Christmastime. Standing on the stoop, with Louise watching through the window, I was carted off by the revelers who placed me on their shoulders and marched down the street to the music. With yells and whoops echoing in my ears, I shouted, "I'm just a little Jewish boy! Weezy..... HEEEEEEEELP!" Louise came bursting out of the house, rushed down the street, white apron fluttering and long legs pumping, and freed me from my captors.

Thank God I had that woman for, by my middle years in elementary school, the family architecture, crumbling at the edges, had been set. Fights between my parents had earned me, at the ripe age of nine, a duodenal ulcer. The barium swallow I had to undergo at Washington Hospital Center made me nauseated. I chewed antacids at school like they were candy. My mother's attempts at turning Deb into a Jewish American Princess was the perfect incentive for Deb to do a 180 on Mom and become a pot-smoking, non-Jew-dating rebel. Lisa, so smart and full of life, didn't fully comprehend the seriousness of her illness. She strained against the hearing aids and low-sugar diet imposed upon her like a horse at the bit. She took on life full force, devouring books, friends, doctors, neighbors, strangers, and any obstacles in her path. She was like a hurricane ~ loud, sharp-tempered, angry that she was so different than the other kids who tormented her about her hearing problem and restricted diet. Daniel was just a little boy, a brilliant one, and was able, like me, to take protection under Louise's wing.

Anger in the house seemed to be everywhere ~ between my parents, between my mother and Louise, between Lisa and Deb, and particularly between my mother and me. On the surface, the strain of an unhappy marriage, a sick child, and unfulfilled expectations must have made her snap. This creative, bohemian spirit of Somerset had become an angry, bitter, envious creature, quick with a scream or, at times, a strap. Certainly there were old scars ~ rumors of an unfaithful father and abandonment while her mother was ill and her father back in Philadelphia. A child of the Great Depression, my mother told me that she needed cardboard to reinforce the bottom of her shoes during those times. There's no denying that her childhood was rough. She told me that while in Palestine she endured a childhood of fear, insecurity, discomfort, and poverty. I have no doubt that this augmented my mother's later struggles with depression, anxiety, addiction and chronic pain. Today, I can easily see how a household environment like that keeps therapists with full schedules.

By the summer of 1966, I had done my time at Camp Airy and returned home to find that my parents had embarked on a six-week tour of Europe, perhaps to salvage their marriage. (The reports we later got from their traveling companions, our cousins Belle and Bob, were that they fought constantly.) That left all four of us kids with Louise as caretaker for about four weeks. The letters we wrote to our parents that summer are telling:

August 8th, 1966
Dear Mom and Dad,

Sorry I couldn't write to you in camp. Are you having fun in Europe? What's it like?

Everyone is fine and Lisa's diabetes is well under control, and she hardly ever spills sugar. Danny has really grown. So has Fredrico Fellini. (Our dachshund, Freddie.) David is still a big baby and is going to need a lot of discipline. I lost 2 pounds. I'm getting on a little better with Lisa, and maybe if I ignore her she'll ignore me.

Love,
Deb

In the margins of the same letter, Louise writes:

Hav (sic) a good time and take your rest, Mrs (sic) Sherer. Louise.

And:

August 12th, 1966
Dear Mom and Dad,

I miss you very much. Have you got something for me? I am lonesome because I don't have any friends. My sugar is still a little high in the morning, but it should and it is always down at chow-time. I am taking 10 of regular and 20 of NPH (insulin) since Dr. Rice changed my dosage. Dad, my acetone was slight this morning. Please do not worry because it is normal to have acetone once in a while! I have a lot of fun with the household, but Debbie never plays with me, only with David or that baby Daniel! I am mad at her because she hardly pays any attention to me.

I only have a toad I carry, but let him go. By the way, Pop, when you want to buy me something here is what I want ~ make your selection, but don't forget my hamster or white mice:

1. moccasin shoes
2. a foreign present from Europe
3. a painting set
4. and an umbrella tent.

Love and kisses,
Lisa

And:

August 2nd, 1966
Dear Mom and Dad,

How are you feeling? I hope you are having a lot of fun. In camp I went to Hershey, Pa. It was a lot of fun. I am having a lot of fun with Weezy.
Please get me something in Israel.

Love,
Dave

When they returned from Europe, my parents prepared us for the upcoming school year, and I was looking forward to a new year of athletics. Indeed, if it hadn't been for sports as an outlet, I probably would have ended up on drugs, in prison, or dead. I was a big kid by fifth grade and did all the sports. Football, soccer, basketball, baseball, golf...I swear they saved my life, keeping me the hell out of the house long enough to avoid the cross fire.

It wasn't only the game, the competition, the fun, the thrill, the challenge, the camaraderie of sport that was my salvation, it was also what went along with it. The odor of a new cotton football jersey as you pulled it over your head for the first time in the early fall; the smell of the rubberized, silk-screened numbers on the front and back; the new teeth guard you had to melt in boiling water to allow it to soften and conform to your mouth; the shiny, black football cleats, size ten by that time, laced tightly to your feet. Fresh out of school at 3:00 p.m. (on non-Hebrew school days), I could not wait to get outside and roam the neighborhood with my new leather Wilson "Duke" football (forty-five dollars at The Sportsman in Bethesda), looking for a game. Next door was a hotspot as we gathered enough kids for a pick-up game, the strains of Bach and Schubert and Chopin wafting down like descending leaves from Mom's piano through the open window facing the lawn. The brilliant oranges and reds from the trees, the soft chill of the autumn breeze, distilled themselves into the almost narcotic feelings that welled up inside me.

As daylight crept away on those late afternoons, each kid, one by one, wandered home. Weezy would be making dinner in the kitchen, her predictable post at that hour. With daylight all but gone, I'd run into the house, grass stains on my bottom and knees, up to the kitchen where the fried chicken would be bubbling in the huge skillet. She'd make my combination salad of iceberg lettuce, cherry tomatoes, cucumbers, and processed cheese croutons, all topped off with Wish-Bone Italian Dressing. I'd throw my arms around her, plant my face in her neck, and inhale all the smells: Noxema, Crisco, frying potatoes, Jheri curl. What intoxication! Could a kid be happier?

The weather wasn't always good for sports and, like any child of the 1960s, I was glued to television too much of the time. Louise would watch along with me when she had a few minutes, and her reaction to people in the news and television in fascinated and puzzled me. Her opinion of Richard Nixon was deeply held. She would say, "That is one uh-uh-gly man. He don't look as good as my foot." Whenever she saw Nixon on the television, she longed for the days when "the Kennedy mens was in the chair." During the presidential election of 1968, she asked me how many votes were needed to win the "electrical college." I could sense her sensual attraction to the bare-chested Muhammad Ali (Louise still knew him as Cassius Clay), which made me uncomfortable. Weezy was spellbound by nature programs, especially ones that depicted what dinosaurs may have looked like. With her head slightly back and turned to the side, eyes narrowed, she looked on in awe at the screen. When I told her how large they were, she looked at me in disbelief. "Big as this house?" she would exclaim. She couldn't get over the fact that an animal could reach such a size.

It was a historic and violent year in America in 1968. Not only was it an election year, a time of increasing American involvement in Vietnam, a period of unabated illicit drug use and unrest in the country, but Martin Luther King, Jr. was assassinated in April. Blacks began rioting in most of the major U.S. cities, and Washington had some of the worst of it. I could see TV coverage of the looting and chaos that was ensuing a mere five or six miles from my comfortable suburban home. I remember listening to coverage of the riot, riding my bike up my clean, safe suburban street, with my cream-colored Emerson transistor radio with brown leatherette case and single cream-colored ear plug shoved in my ear, and thinking how the rioters' hero and leader had been viciously gunned down. Louise was afraid to go down to Friendship Heights at the District Line (and we were afraid to take her), so she stayed home the Thursday and Saturday of the week that the rioting was the worst, April fourth through the eighth. Many Jewish merchants who owned food markets, liquor stores, and shops in DC were afraid for their businesses, but there were a few who were spared supposedly because of favorable treatment of blacks. Others did not do so well. It was a bad time for everyone in DC.

When the dust has settled and things got back to relative normalcy in Washington, a parallel calming of the waters was taking a tentative hold in my own home.

Chapter Five

House of Cards

ထဝၺ

Bethesda, Maryland
1969-1976

From late childhood to my early teen years, a tenuous equilibrium of sorts was reached at 8520 West Howell Road. My parents ran hot and cold ~ hot with fighting and cold with affection. Deb became increasingly desirous of being anywhere but in the house, and Lisa pushed on in school, eventually gaining some modicum of control over her disease. I had sports and the piano that I had started studying in the sixth grade, and Daniel was busy being a Lego master and young literary genius. As early as age seven, he wrote poetry and even a few plays, one fancifully called the *Emerald Connection* and another entitled *Setting* in which he lambasted my mother and satirized the scam of the relationship that my parents endured. Sadly, things were increasingly not good enough for my mother. She insisted on owning a double oven (even though she practically could not boil water) and chided my father on his choice of loud, outdated clothing, mid-level cars, and the fact that we did not belong to a country club.

Fortunately, my parents, by the time I was eleven, exerted two profound and lasting influences on me that continue to this day ~ the disparate disciplines of classical piano and golf. My mother had been a talented pianist since her middle childhood, and I have early memories of sucking on the milk bottle under the baby grand in the living room on Colston Drive in Silver Spring to the clatter of Schubert and Bach above my head. By sixth grade, it was time to find a suitable teacher, my mother decided. Upon recommendation of her playing partner, Joan Hollander, Mom decided on the well-known and ancient British taskmaster, Katherine Frost, whose home and teaching studio was situated near elegant Embassy Row, on Phelps Place, NW, one of the best addresses in DC.

So, it began. After a full day of school, once a week and on a day that I wasn't tortured at Hebrew school, my mother would drive me downtown and drop me off for my one-hour lesson. A knock on the huge front portico, an eternity, an adagio rotation of the crystal doorknob, and the recession of the equally grand door gave way to the intimidating presence that was Mrs. Katherine Frost. I was led to the performance podium, where, like two moored, oily, black battleships, her twin Steinway Concert Grand pianos stood side by side.

With skin as frail as tissue paper and seemingly so old that Moses Himself was probably in her yearbook, she would teach strictly and severely. Rapping my fingers with her long, red string-wrapped crayon-pencil, she would warn, in her clipped British accent: "Your parents are wasting precious cash. Now, if you DON'T count, I shall simply have to throw you out!" One time I got so flustered and unnerved about asking to use the bathroom for fear of wasting both time and "precious cash" that, unable to hold it in any longer, I urinated all over myself and her black leather piano bench.

My studies with her lasted about a year, at which time I was able to negotiate, with my mother as ambassador, a respectable exit, with the excuse that my upcoming Bar Mitzvah study requirements necessitated a temporary hold my piano pedagogy. I still have sheet music from that time, hidden facedown in a secluded drawer, riddled with her red crayon scrawl.

I tried in those years to avoid my mother's wrath and apparent unhappiness, and I grew closer to my father who had first introduced me to golf at age ten. By then, my father and I were bonding more strongly as we had settled into a routine that would last well into my late teens. Every Saturday morning he would take me on hospital rounds with him where he'd make me wait at the nurses' station while he examined patients in their rooms. I got to know a lot of the staff at two hospitals over the years, and I delighted in spinning the chart carousel around, sneaking the always-present chocolates that seem to hide in and around where the nurses and clerks congregated, and fiddle with the stickers that read "No BM Today" or "NPO for Surgery" or "Fall Precaution." Sometimes I'd stick the "No BM Today" sticker on my forehead and wait for my father to return from a patient's room. He gave me that half smile, called me a character, shook his head, and then if the patient wasn't too sick, would let me in the room and introduce me as his junior associate. I got to know quite a few of his patients over the years and would ask about them often. I remember one man in particular who suffered for years with chronic, intermittent hiccups. It astounded me that any one individual could suffer that long with something that annoying. Almost all of his patients and the hospital staff seemed to say the same thing about me: "You look just like your father." That made me a bit embarrassed but somewhat proud as well.

I didn't always like going into patients' rooms. Dad usually shielded me from some of the sicker people, but occasionally I would see things I wish I hadn't, like tubes in the patients' nostrils sucking out some brown liquid, a urinary catheter with a bag hanging by the bedside filled with blood-tinged urine, or IVs dripping all kinds of different liquids of varying hues into people. I came to the conclusion early in life that sick people and sickness were entities unattractive but, when not self-inflicted from obesity, smoking, etc., deserving of the deepest sympathy. That attitude would influence my later relationship with Lisa as well as my concern for her. On a profound level, these images had a lasting effect on my attitudes toward my eventual profession.

After rounds at the hospital, we would, in temperate seasons, head to the golf course. My father took up the game later in life, in his forties, but rapidly became quite a good golfer. He later claimed that golf was such a great diversion for him that it, like Tegretol, added years to his life. He played regularly up until six months before he died at the age of eighty-seven. Although he taught me almost everything I know about the game, he wasn't the ideal playing partner. To the contrary, his constant boasting about my skills on the course led me to be overly self-conscious. This carried over into other areas of my life, as Dad did not merely leave the bragging to my golfing ability. He would go on about how big my feet were, how far I could hit a baseball, how well

I could play the piano, and how fast I was on the football field. By putting this extra pressure on me, I developed some pretty bad performance anxiety that, for an already sensitive and nervous kid, was a destructive combination. I dreaded when we'd have to team up with strangers on the golf course because before I could even get up to the first tee, he was already starting with his: "Wait you see how this kid hits the ball" and "How come ya hit it so short" if I split the fairway with a 240-yard drive. He really did me a disservice.

Though a habitual exaggerator, Dad had his admirable qualities. One was his empathy. Others were his intellect and his breadth of knowledge. His interests in science, history, music, and literature were voracious, and he kept these habits up until his last years.

When not spending time with my father, I had Louise to fill the void left by my mother's inflexible attitudes and her temper, criticisms, and overbearing opinions: "You don't want to go to Hebrew school, David? Fine! But you can forget about playing football!" Or: "You only are going to date Jewish girls, aren't you?" Or, the old favorite: "If you don't become a doctor you could always sell shoes." This drove me closer to Louise who represented, more and more, what my mother was not: self-effacing, patient, calm, soft-spoken, kind, and poor.

This juxtaposition of personalities left me confused. A triad of parents: two females, one male, two races, all of them complex in ways that both unsettled and intrigued me. As the bickering between the two women and between my natural parents grew, my sense of self, security, and confidence necessarily suffered. It got so bad that many times during any given year the fights between my parents or my mother and Weezy would compel her to pack all her belongings and disappear for a few days only to return after some sort of reconciliation. These were particularly wrenching for me, and I can remember sitting on Louise's old trunk in her basement room, tears running down my face, imploring her to stay. "Yo' momma is just crazy," she'd say, looking off in the distance at nowhere in particular. I asked her where she would go, but she never gave me a straight answer. "Chester and me might find a place over yonder somewhere in DC," she'd say, but I never knew where that was. "Anyway, yo' momma and me just don't get along." I never knew after the first few times this would happen when the real break would come, but I was so relieved each time my father would get the message to pick her up at the District Line and bring her home.

What they bickered over seemed so trivial. Even young Danny was made privy to it. Here are a few typical exchanges:

Danny: "Everything bothers Mom these days!"

Weezy: "I know it. What's the matter with her? She made herself like that, complainin' all the time."

Danny: "That's right!"

Weezy: "Pickin' out things to complain about, sayin' how much money Lo-retta (as she called my father's more showy cousin, Loretta, who lived in tony Potomac) and Bob (her doctor husband) makes and all this bullshit...."

Or:

Weezy: "Yo' momma say that I bother her cause I pop my gum so loud. Where is it but around the house that I'm gonna chew gum? Huh! She the one who done snap and pop her gum! She can snap and pop her gum 'most as loud as any person I know."

And:

Mom: "Louise, do me a favor. When you get off the phone, go into the carport and bring me in those bags of ice I left in the cooler for the party, and do it soon before they melt! PLEASE? I got a lot a things to do before these damn folks come over. Off the phone, NOW, PLEASE!"

Louise: "You cain't talk to me like that! I'se growed! I get it befo' long; hit won't melt..."

Or:

Weezy: "Miss Lady done called and said for you to call her back."

Mom: "Who in the HELL is Miss Lady? Oh, my back hurts! Please, Louise, can't you tell me?"

Louise: "You know, she married to, what do you call him, Mr. Man? I cain't quite 'call the name.... They live over yonder. Oh! Mrs. Yunker!"

Mom: "Who?"

Louise: "You know, Mrs. YUNKER!"

Mom: "Mrs. YON-ker. Oh! Well, why didn't you tell me? And since David's not here, can you come upstairs and pull on my leg while I lie down? My back and leg hurt like hell!"

###

In my preteen years, I was not the only child drawn to Weezy's charms and humor. By the time Daniel became old enough to appreciate Louise's specialness, he took it upon himself to document, for all time, her personality, speech, and mannerisms. One way he did this was to record her, on tape, surreptitiously and overtly, in candid and often "set-up" conversations. These eventually became the now infamous "Weezy Tapes" that Daniel codified in The Archives. The Archives, collected over a period of decades, contain photographs, recordings, various written documents, family-crafted works of art, original works of literature, and even an encoded language created by Daniel himself. These are all stored in an old wooden chest up in the room that Daniel and I shared as children. Always a boy of ritual, Daniel would insist upon the shaking of a ceremonial rattle ~ a West African basket contraption filled with beads ~ before opening The Archives. He loosened up on that in his adult years.

Decades later, my rehearing of these tapes revealed much about Louise's mindset, her growing resentments toward my mother, her illogical fear of my father, and her attitudes toward herself and other members of my family. I came to see that, behind the bickering, was this: a deep sense on Louise's part that while she had nothing, my mother had virtually anything a person could ask for. And yet, it was my mother, albeit with a sick child and myriad problems of her own, who was always complaining, always unhappy, and always "raisin' a fuss." To a dirt-poor black woman from Macon, Georgia who had given up one kid for adoption and could only see her other child for mere hours during the week, she had to have harbored ill feelings toward her employer.

###

By the end of elementary school and the start junior high, I had become a respectable athlete, doing well in baseball, basketball, and football. In the spring of 1969, I played baseball for the Burning Tree Indians and, still self-conscious from what my dad did to me on the golf course, made for a poor fielder. I thought I would assuredly muff up catching the ball and be incapable of throwing it accurately. That's why they put me at first base, a position where I would do the least damage. Happily, this didn't carry over into my batting, where I excelled. In fact, I tied for the most home runs that year with Roy, our catcher.

Playing for the Indians, my best friends among us, was fun beyond description. Donald Call, or D.B. to everyone who knew and revered him, was the coolest kid in school. With flaming red hair, freckles, and a derring-do that was a synthesis of James Bond and Cool Hand Luke, he was the idol of sixth grade. He knew about firecrackers, motorcycles, booze, and, especially, girls. D.B.'s father, John, coached us that year, and everyone called him by his nickname, "Gracks." I used a very heavy bat that year, and Gracks called it my "Irish shillelagh." Since my last name was Sherer, he called me "Shiree," and I knew I was one of his favorite players because of my batting and my sense of humor. He was constantly in arguments with opposing teams' coaches and spectators who accused me of being a ringer because of my size. The age limit on that team was thirteen, and I was so big that everyone would badger Gracks about whether I met the playing criteria. This got him so upset that at one point he screamed out, "Goddammit! The kid ain't even Bar Mitzvahed yet!' We all thought this was hysterical, especially coming from a Quaker.

In seventh and eighth grade I played basketball for the Pyle Panthers. I started at forward that first year and had uncanny skill shooting long shots from the corners along the baseline but suffered from a significant "choke" curse, missing easy layups and shots from close in. This recurring trait of making the tough seem easy and the easy tough was a vestige of my father's influence. I loved the feeling of being watched by the cheerleaders who chanted my name: "Sheer, Sheer, he's our man, if he can't do it," so-and-so can. The frenzy and adrenaline rush that came with running up and down the court knowing that I would be watched by parents, fellow students, and especially girls was a sensation few of us get in adulthood.

In eighth grade one game stood out. While playing against Hoover Junior High School in Bethesda, I came up against an African American center who sported a beard, chest hair, and looked like he could have had three kids. Those Hoover guys had uniforms fancy enough to have their names on the back of the jerseys, and I remember his last name to this day: Imes. He was like a bull, probably weighed 230 pounds, was over six feet tall, and whether he was fourteen years old like the rest of us was anybody's guess. I had no chance against this man-child as he boxed me out on play after play, tossing me aside with his body like a bowling ball knocking over a pin. I really thought it unfair that a guy who could have three children and had a beard could be put up against the hardly pubescent Jewish boys like me.

Although painfully shy with girls, I remained the class clown, and, continuing my elementary school tradition, earned myself a memorialized seat outside the principal's office. Although I desperately wanted a girlfriend and was as horny as Lisa's blood-squirting toad, I never overcame the shyness and guilt fostered in me by my parents, especially my mother. (Jewish guilt, in my opinion, is peripherally related to Catholic guilt, only more matured, slow-cooked, and looser on the bone. Being Catholic guilt's older brother, it is more insidious and gradual, the latter more abrupt and convenient to assuage with confession, indulgences, and the like.) Actually, at age thirteen, "guilty" should have been my middle name. Guilty that I could not stop my parents from fighting or cure Lisa's hearing problems and diabetes or make Mom and Louise get along better or make Deb not so rebellious and reeking of reefer when she came home or get prepared quickly enough for my impending Bar Mitzvah or become the golden-Jew-boy doctor soon enough who made all things better for Danny.

Mom made sure of that.

How did she make sure? She was a virtual travel agent for guilt trips, that's how. It was and is still common in the DC suburbs for diplomatic staff and their families to rent houses in the upper-class neighborhoods for their two- to three-year stints in the nation's capital, and one house our street fit the bill. One such family was from South America, consisting of two parents and their children, two boys and one girl. Their manner of dress was bit "off" to my preteen American tastes, and they referred to soccer as "football." The girl, Adrianna, was very pretty, with long brown hair and a great figure. One afternoon I came into the house and told my mother that I had been speaking with Adrianna about some fellow schoolmates who Adrianna had seen kissing. My mother must have misunderstood me, thinking that I said that Adrianna and I had been kissing. All of a sudden she got hysterical and shrilly blurt, "You weren't kissing Adrianna, were you!? "No, Ma!" I entreated, "it was Adrianna telling me about the other students!" I felt so shitty. What should she care if I did kiss Adrianna, anyway?

Louise had her own opinions of my looks and prospects with girls. "Them girls is going to have a taffy-pullin' contest over you," she'd say, but sadly, that didn't seem to represent reality. No matter. She continued to heap praise upon me. One day it would be over my ability at the piano, another day it was my schoolwork. "You is the most intelligent boy in the whole world," she would exclaim. She frequently would bless me by asking me to stop whatever I was doing and, placing her hands firmly on the crown of my head, incant, "Heavenly Father, bless this boy from the top of his head to the bottom of his foots. Have all power in your hand, heavenly Father, and give him as much faith as a mustard seed...for we don't know the seasons but for the buddin' of the trees...." What this all meant and the sources of its varied biblical origins, I wasn't entirely acquainted with, but it certainly was more praise and encouragement that I ever received from my mother. After she'd finished her blessing, she'd back away and insist, "I better let you get your lesson! You sho' is smart." I thanked her with a hug and a kiss on her ebony, silken cheek and got back to whatever I was doing, realizing that at least someone was satisfied with me just as me.

I swear the woman saved my life.

Opposing forces dominated my early teenage life. I was lucky to have sports, friends, and golf with my father. But piano lessons with an ancient and repressive tyrant, Hebrew school, constant tension at home between my parents, and my mother's worsening temper outbursts and illnesses wore me down. One afternoon, my brother and I were playing chess in the Gorgeous when she arrived home with groceries in the station wagon. She honked the horn as a signal for us to get up to help bring them inside. When we didn't immediately leap to our feet, she came screaming into the room and with a broad sweep of her arm knocked all the quartz chess pieces across the room. "Goddammit," she said, "when I say get the groceries I mean: GET THE FUCKING GROCERIES!" Today, if one looked carefully enough, shards of quartz knights, bishops, and rooks could probably be found interred in the vomit-green shag rug that still adorns the floor of that room.

In fairness, my mother did have a lot to contend with. Chronic pain became her tormentor, and multiple failed back surgeries further embittered her. For the better part of twenty years, she was ill-tempered and bed-ridden, relying on traction devices and me to literally pull her leg to relieve the pressure on her lumbar nerve roots. I can remember the hospital bed in her room and the Demerol pills and injections she was taking. My father was even supplying her with them.

I began to notice a change in Louise as well. The generalized insanity going on in the household must have metastasized, and her behavior took on a bizarre, even mystical quality, reflected even in her lodgings. Her room was in the basement of our home, the drabness of which could not go unnoticed. It was small and narrow, about the size of my dad's office examining room, and it smelled of mothballs and Noxema. Against the wall was wedged a single bed, opposite of which resided a dresser with narrow tabletop and a mirror. On the tabletop sat her compact leather-covered Bible, bookmarked with its built-in purple silk ribbon. Her simple, black, horn-rimmed reading glasses lay on top of the book. To the side of the dresser sat Louise's massive, mysterious black trunk finished with pebbled, tough plastic and with two massive brass bolts and a brass keyhole. There was a single chair. A closet door with unpainted wooden slats was at the left as one entered. There were no pictures on the walls, no photographs except for the single yearly calendar from the Harvest Spiritual Church suspended by a meek and lonely red thumbtack. A McDonald's Hamburglar doll hung on the wall with flowers adorning it. On the small dresser opposite her bed sat a candle about six inches tall with the circumference of a silver dollar and with hieroglyphic symbols running the length of it. That was the "Egyptian Money Gettin' candle" Louise had made mention of. Around the room were small handwritten notes in Louise's large, firm handwriting; I could never decipher their meaning.

I would often go down to check on her and find her with her glasses on, head bowed, and her mouthing words from the New Testament. Here's a typical exchange:

"Hi, Weezy, can I come in?"

"Sho', old man!"

"Are you feelin' alright? Can I get you a Co-Cola?," I'd ask, speaking her language.

"Naw," she'd answer, "Jes' promise me one thang. When I'm an old lady, hoppin' on a stick, will you take care of me? Take care of the Old Chocolate Lady?'

"Sure I will, Wee."

She'd smile, give me a hug, and we'd both laugh.

I didn't have the nerve to ask about the Hamburglar doll or candle.

###

Around this time, my father was starting what would become a multiyear depression. A sick wife and daughter, trigeminal neuralgia, and the stress of practice and economic demands were exacting a toll. Added to this was the start of a frivolous malpractice lawsuit that, after many years, would eventually be thrown out of court. The photographs from that time are shocking. My father went from a burly 230 pounds to 165 pounds in the span of six months. He looked like a cancer victim. Everything took on a dour tone, and Louise's cooking repulsed him. He again half-jokingly accused her of trying to kill him with her nightly fare.

His behavior became more worrisome, as well. He had a collection of pistols and rifles that he had bought years before for target shooting on our farm in Manassas, Virginia. During this period of depression, he would sit in front of the television with his fearsome .357 Magnum and shoot the unloaded monster at the screen. This got me and my mother so worried that one day we took up all the weapons and went to Irving Sporting Goods in Silver Spring, Maryland and sold them all. When he discovered this I was surprised by his reaction. Instead of one of his famous outbursts he shrugged it off. The depression must have knocked the fight out of him.

###

In the early 1970s, my mother's mother moved in with us. Suffering from serious heart ailments, she was no longer able to care for herself, and my father assumed some of her medical care. Louise assumed some of her nursing care as well. Hannah or "Safta," the Hebrew name for "grandmother," was about the palest woman I ever saw. She exuded illness. She was in her mid-seventies when she moved in with us but looked twenty years older. Her cardiologist described her chest x-ray as supporting the largest heart diameter he had ever seen. (Years later, when I was in medical school, I put eyes on the film myself. The cardiac shadow indeed was enormous, an indication of the severe congestive heart failure that would trouble her the rest of her life.) Her skin was virtually transparent, she emitted all sorts of strange sounds, and, to my less-than-mature adolescent eyes, moved slowly through the house like an anemic Titanic, waiting for one of her ailments to sink her. Her teeth were kept in a glass by the bed. A stifling, dour presence, she was always looking on the bad side of things and irritated at my apparent disinterest in religious study and my fondness for sports, which she collectively referred to as "ball." The only joy I was able to give her was my learning to read Yiddish from *The Jewish Daily Forwards*, the prominent Yiddish language newspaper.

Her thick Eastern European accent made quite an impression on Louise who heard her speak Yiddish with my mother. For instance, the word "gutinyu" can be loosely translated as "oh my God," and Louise appropriated it for her own use as "gutin-*me*." Louise called her "Sotta," and the interaction between them caused my brother and me much amusement. Safta called Weezy "Lou-eesse" (pronounced like who-is), and if it weren't for Louise's sheer physical strength and dedication, I doubt Safta would have been able to bathe or even live as long as she did. In the end, it seemed a fair deal ~ nursing care in exchange for lessons in Yiddish and elementary Jewish traditions.

Other than helping with her activities of daily living, Louise had not much to say to Hannah, let alone do with her. It wasn't out of dislike or prejudice on Hannah's part; it was just a fact. My grandmother spent most of her time reading, sewing, sleeping, or playing with Danny ~ whom she favored over me ~ and rightly so. Daniel had little interest in "ball" and, being younger and better behaved, was easier to deal with than me: the teenage, ball-playing, piano-banging "vilde chaya" (wild animal, in Yiddish). Besides, Daniel was a cleaner slate, a new specimen to imprint with quiet, polite behavior and Jewish traditions and language.

By thirteen, every self-respecting Jewish boy, from the most radically bereft Reform to the holiest rolling Orthodox, is expected to become a man in the eyes of the Jewish community, and since our degree of devotion fell smack in the middle, that is, the Conservative branch of American Judaism, that meant my time had come. All those tedious and tortuous years in Hebrew school (Mondays and Wednesdays after regular school and Sunday mornings as well) and those Rosh Hashanah and Yom Kippur (New Year's and Day of Atonement) services were to culminate at my Bar Mitzvah, the ceremony marking my arrival into manhood in the Jewish faith, scheduled for June 6th, 1970.

My views, by that time, of religion in general and services in particular were not exactly sanguine. My mother used to force me to go to synagogue on Saturday mornings and sometimes my father would accompany us. Usually he would be so exhausted from the stresses of the week that he would be asleep within about ten minutes. Whenever he would wake up he'd look over at me with one eye open and mumble something about how this is so much "bullshit" and that all religion was based on fear. I detested being inside the synagogue while the weather was so nice outside.

Whenever I was sentenced to the kids' service, which was separate from the main auditorium, I would sneak down to the boiler room to hang out with the black janitors who made it their refuge. I remember two janitors in particular, each with a white and red oval name patch sewn into his blue shirts. One was named Dan, a huge, lumbering man who must have been seriously ill although I didn't realize it at the time. His English was almost unintelligible, and he must have been six-five and weighed well over 300 pounds. The other was named Willie, who played Mutt to Dan's Jeff, and he looked like what you might imagine to be the stereotypic Nation of Islam member from those days. He was fairly light-skinned, slender, with a pencil-thin mustache, bow tie, and sarcastic demeanor. He resembled a kind of black Dick Powell. He often mocked me by speaking gibberish, which was either an imitation of our Hebrew incantations or something to do with the Nation of Islam or some conglomeration of the two. I never found out which. Despite his sarcasm, I endured his company and preferred it to going to services. (Was it part of my Jewish guilt for what I perceived Louise had to endure and sacrifice?)

When my grandmother and mother found out that I had been hanging out in the boiler room with the janitors instead of attending the services for the kids, they practically lost their latkes. They couldn't accept that I preferred the company of black janitors to listening to a language I didn't understand in clothes that chaffed in the company of people I found so serious and severe.

On Saturday afternoon, June 6th, 1970, in a special afternoon ceremony (the Mincha Maariv service) that occurs only rarely in the Jewish yearly calendar, I became a Bar Mitzvah. Hundreds of people ~ relatives, friends, and most conspicuously Louise ~ came to see me in my white pinstripe Cricketeer jacket, navy blue shirt, and white silk tie with gold tiepin. I was an utter wreck. I had had stomach pains since fourth grade (Weezy called them "scrapes in the stomach") because of my parents' fighting and because I felt so insecure about who I was and whether Weezy would leave the family. But by that day, my stomach hurt me so badly that I didn't think I would able to go on. Chewing Maalox tablets like they were mints, I stood on the "bema" (raised platform), my mouth so dry that it sounded like a croaking frog in my own head, and somehow powered my way through the service. To keep myself grounded, I focused my attention on the traditional handheld silver pointer with the miniature hand on the end that guided one's reading in the Torah.

The reception was a blur: a long line, people stuffing envelopes in my pocket, a short blessing over the bread and wine, the Gene Donati Orchestra, food, drinks, odors of onion-tinged bad breath and armpit sweat, a photo session, my friends cavorting in the basement of the synagogue, and two pretty girls in my lap (Sally and Debbie) with me trying to suppress a boner.

Although I had finally become "a man," I was so spent they had to take me home early from my own Bar Mitzvah.

By seventh grade, my thirteenth year, my older sisters were well into their middle teens and off in their own worlds of boyfriends, growing independence, and dodging my parents'

The author, class clown of seventh grade.

oversight. Hippie stuff was everwhere: tie-dyed shirts, bell bottoms, Hendrix and Joplin albums, pot, pipes, rolling paper, Peter Max posters, patchouli perfume and 45 rpm records.

When I wasn't occupied by sports or the piano, this left Danny and me, sharing the uppermost upstairs bedroom, more time together to interact with each other and Louise. Sometimes these interactions got us into trouble, such as the time the newly corrupted Danny and I made the mistake of sneaking into the den, closing the door, and getting caught doing something that has probably condemned us for all eternity to Judaic Hell (even though none exists in our faith.) Once safely ensconced, we turned on any number of sitcoms ~ *McHale's Navy*, *The Andy Griffith Show*, or *I Love Lucy* ~ and turned the sound off the television. Then, while turning on my Bar Mitzvah practice tapes on the tape recorder, we synchronized holy Jewish prayers to the moving lips on the screen. For example, we were able to take my Torah reading and watch Aunt Bea, Captain Binghamton, Barney Fife, or fat Fred Mertz mouth out holy Hebrew scripture from thousands of years ago. Cackling and unbridled laughter emanated from the den. Slowly, the den door creaked open. It was Safta. Visibly shaking with a mixture of rage and shame, she screamed, "Vat are you? Cookoo!? Dat's de 'Oliest of Olies! Make it OFF! Vat are you, crazy?! SHADDUP!" She looked like she was either going to kill us or have a heart attack or both.

Not all of our joint activities were so utterly bankrupt of dignity and respect. Every day after school, when Daniel was in elementary school, he would come home and immerse himself in *The World Book Encyclopedia*. After he had finished that, he graduated to *The Encyclopedia Britannica* where he, quite literally, garnered his encyclopedic range of knowledge. It became our tradition at bedtime that he and I played a game we called "World Book Quiz Game" in which we would test each other about the beginning face page of an article in *The World Book* and what the page featured as far as figures or photographs and/or what the first few words of the article were.

Daniel was also a master architect and builder of Lego. But instead of building normal Lego constructions like most children, Daniel appropriated bits and pieces of household items like sticks, rubber bands, kitchen items, and other any other paraphernalia he could gather to make some of his special creations. One such machine he called the P'Boinsk that was an elaborately designed contraption made with Lego and rubber bands that would explode in an orgiastic frenzy when a certain Lego piece was pressed. He even built a working model of Louise out of Lego, complete with movable jaws. He would take one of the many tape recordings that he had of Louise and would move the jaws back and forth in synchrony to her taped speech: "Dan-yu! Pick up yo' room" or "Danyu, yo momma say 'come there!'" Small wonder that my brother, Daniel C. Sherer, eventually got a Ph.D. in art history at Harvard and now teaches at Yale, Columbia, and Cooper Union.

My junior high school and high school years passed quickly. I had lots of crushes on girls but never had the guts to ask any of them on a date. I continued on with sports, contributing to our win of the 1971 Capital Beltway Youth League football championship as a member of the Springfield Lions. In a game televised on a local station and announced by Maury Povich, a DC fixture like his late sportswriter father Shirley Povich, I was a standout on both offense and defense, which led me to earn starting positions on the tenth grade Whitman

Vikings JV team, where, after games, Louise would give me alcohol rubdowns (her idea, not mine.) Wrapped to the waist in a towel after a hot shower, I would lie on my bed upstairs and feel Weezy's strong, massive hands massage the cold, pungent liquid into my skin, cognizant of her warning to keep my towel up since she "wasn't supposed to see you nekked."

The steely glare of my father, Max G. Sherer M.D.

I had finally found the right piano teacher, Anthony Chanaka, who had studied with Nadia Boulanger in Paris and, through her, could trace his musical pedigree back to Beethoven. Under his guidance, I became a competent intermediate pianist in the span of three years. My studies at school, however, weren't so great. A low B student, I was the classic underachiever, lacking confidence in my abilities and probably suffering from what today would be labeled a salad of ADD, OCD, and probably some other form of D, with a dash of depression and anxiety for good measure.

In the middle of tenth grade, after a successful football season with the JV Whitman Vikings and struggling as barely a C+ student, my father had the brilliant idea to send me to the elite Sidwell Friends School, institution of the Obama children and Chelsea Clinton. This might have been influenced by the fact that our next-door neighbor had two boys flourishing there. Typically, my father acted impulsively on this decision, giving no consideration that it was already mid-year, I was a mediocre scholar at best, and I would likely crash and burn in a new place with new, smarter students, a much more rigorous curriculum, and a vastly different social structure. But, being the "Great White Jewish Hope" of the family, I was asked to do more and do it better. Committing any number of child-rearing errors, Dad took a Calvinist approach. Indeed, was it not predetermined that I would become a doctor? And since no tenth grader with terrible grades in public school would likely get into a prestigious university or college and then on to medical school, was it not logical and wise that I attend Sidwell?

Part of the decision may have had to do with prestige. To get his oldest son into one of the city's, if not the nation's, finest private schools would be quite the feather in his cap, a great bragging point and a source of unending pride. On that altar, I suppose Abraham was ready to unwittingly sacrifice Isaac. But, unluckily for me, there was no angel to stay his hand.

In the fall of eleventh grade, after my half year of making one A in English and the rest Cs and Ds at Sidwell Friends the prior spring, I was back at Whitman, enduring the taunts of my classmates and trying out for varsity football. "Whatsa' matta, Sheer? Couldn't make it at that fancy private school?" The varsity football coach, Coach Milloy, never gave me the chance I deserved, for he had his hopes set at tight end for now-billionaire mogul Mitchell Rales, a senior both bigger and stronger than myself. Not willing to warm the bench for a year, I told Milloy that if he didn't give me the chance to show my stuff, I would leave the team. His response? "Go play your damn pianny instead, Sheer." I took his advice. I promptly quit the team and got sweet revenge as the 1973 Whitman Football Vikings went 0 and 10.

Louise's sense of justice must have rubbed off on me, and I miraculously found the ability to wield its sword, as with my walkout on the Cub Scouts, when my sense of outrage was stirred enough.

I decided my high school sports days were over.

The school year went by, and things had settled down a little around the house. Louise had taken to preaching on the streets corners in DC and had started to refer to herself as "Elder Morris". She claimed that she had received a calling to do this work and would regale Danny and me with stories of soul saving. One, due to the sheer surreal imagery it evoked, stood out. She was standing on the corner in DC one day when a man approached her. She told me he showed her a "notebook that was full of a picture of a whole pack of old woman's wombs." (Da Vinci's anatomy notebook? Pornography, perhaps?) "'Elder Morris, I got somethin' to show you, and I don't want you to tell NO-body. You know what that is?'" he says. Weezy replies, "'Sho', I know what that is ~ that's the wombs of a woman ~ what about it? I asked him, trying to tell me what that was. The man looked at me so hard he didn't know what to do. Them folks around here is crazy, David. I said, 'Sure I know what that is! That the wombs of a woman!'" (Louise could be quite repetitive.) "What...what... what...what about it, I asked him? 'Stupid-North-Carolina-son-of-a-bitch', I said to myself." I never did learn why Louise held people from the Tar Heel state in such low esteem. Out of the blue, Daniel asked Louise if perhaps the North Carolinians were somehow shell-shocked from the Second World War. Louise replied, "Child, all of them is BORN shell-shock!"

Daniel and I loved these stories and, being a natural historian, Daniel was further encouraged to get as many of Weezy's tales and antics on tape as possible. Daniel's foresight in this regard is a testament to his early genius, and I am forever grateful for what he did in preserving so much of what Louise meant and means to me to this day. In my opinion, the stuff belongs in its own History of Southern American Folk Museum. Or a linguistic museum, at least.

###

Late senior year found me struggling academically, insecure emotionally, without a girlfriend, and naïve in almost every sense except musically where my piano studies developed to the point where I was playing Chopin études, Beethoven's Piano Concerto No. 1, and Schumann's Papillion. It was, of course, still understood that I was going to follow my father's path and become a doctor, but I had not the first idea what lay ahead other than college. I knew I was not ready to live away from home as the memories of Camp Airy hung over my head like some sort of magical, homesickness-conjuring Sword of Damocles, along with all the emotional insecurities that made their way into my psyche.

So, with my head lodged firmly up my ass, I hauled myself down to the Walt Whitman High School guidance counselor's office to find out about admission to college. Those times were so different than now. Few, if any, essays, letters of recommendation, or information other than your GPA and SAT scores were required, at least for application to in-state schools. There was none of these highfalutin' "why I want to go to Princeton" essay, community service, captain of the fencing team, and DNA-sampling nonsense that goes on today.

The logical option for me at the time, a low B student with mediocre SAT scores, was application to the University of Maryland in College Park. I filled out the forms then and there, in Counselor Shuma's office. It took me all of ten minutes. I was told, as I handed the paper into his pudgy paw that barring any unanticipated malfeasance in behavior or academic performance in the few weeks left of high school I could expect my acceptance letter by the end of the school year.

Three weeks later, I was a Maryland Terrapin.

After a summer working at Giant Food as a cashier at their Friendship Heights store (five bucks an hour was a lot of dough in the summer of '75) and unsuccessfully making time in my father's 1972 brown Buick Centurion convertible with the older, more worldly female cashiers, (my mother warned: "wait 'til they get you between their legs!") I began school August 28th. I lived at home that freshman year, studied hard, yearned in vain for a girlfriend (although I was still too shy and insecure to get one), and proceeded to make straight As. What caused the academic turnaround was the surprisingly excellent teaching, a true interest in the coursework, and the underlying fear and realization that, if I didn't do well, I would never get the grades and confidence to finally leave home for good. After being lectured to by my personal physician as to the importance of leaving home ~ especially my home since he knew my parents well ~ I mustered the strength that late winter to apply for transfer.

That's when my association with Louise's home state, the great state of Georgia, began.

Chapter Six

Homes Away from Home and Visits Home

ಬಂಞಿ

Atlanta, Georgia; Boston, Massachusetts; and Miami, Florida
1976-1989

In 1976, Emory University was a popular choice for undergraduate education, especially for premed students at Whitman High School in Bethesda, Maryland and in the Northeast of the country. It gained that reputation like the other "Harvards of the South"~ Duke, Vanderbilt, and William and Mary ~ due to its reliable record of getting graduating seniors into medical school and law school. For some reason, Emory had been able to put a foothold at Whitman those few years, and, by all accounts, still does so today. To transfer away from the University of Maryland and break the umbilical cord, my choices came down to Emory and Purdue, where my uncle was a professor of chemistry. Despite my fondness for my uncle, I chose Emory. The fact that Louise was from Georgia and her sister, Susie, lived in Atlanta didn't hurt either. Eventually, I feel it proved to be the right decision.

As a transfer student, I missed out on on-campus housing and took up a studio apartment, complete with faux leopard love seat, wooden desk and chair, toilet, shower, and refrigerator, across from the Emory University Law School at 1785 N. Decatur Road. Homesick and insecure, I soon met my first real girlfriend, a Methodist minister's daughter. As we got to know each other, she heard quite a few Weezy stories as did many of the friends I made, so that today, thirty-seven years later, many of them still ask me about Louise and can recount verbatim some of her stock phrases that had become so famous. One summer my girlfriend, Deborah, had taken an internship to work in the office of Senator Hollings of South Carolina in Washington, DC, and that gave her an opportunity to finally meet Louise. After taking her back to her lodgings that evening, I returned home to find that Louise had issued judgment on my first real girlfriend: "There ain't nothing wrong with her looks; and she got itty-bitty foots, too!" Evidently, foot size to Louise, perhaps over any other bodily feature, was an important criterion for attractiveness, and my girlfriend had passed one of Louise's critical tests of beauty.

That relationship didn't last through college, but Louise continued to play cheerleader on my chances with women. On visits home or on the phone from Atlanta, I was heartened by Weezy's outlook: "Them girls is goin' to pull you apart." Or, if had broken up with one: "Go on about your business and get you another one."

Visits home during college naturally led me to discuss Atlanta with Louise, and Daniel missed no chance in capturing this and other more revealing stories on cassette tape. What Louise poured out was, to me, pure, historical, twenty-four-carat gold. In a 1977 exchange between us, she recounts how things were in Atlanta when she was a younger working woman. Louise describes how Atlanta could be "the roughest place you ever seen in your life" and that "people were scared to get off the train, there was so much going on."

There was Mitchell Street, where people would be "carrying switchblade knives and threaten you just with their looks." "Womens would run from the bus or train as fast as they could to not let the crooks and dope dealers cut they handbags away." She said that she "didn't pay them no attention," however, and that they didn't even bother her because she was a "holy woman" and that God protected her. "Everybody said Atlanta was a good place. Parts of there is rough, too! You don't go messin' downtown there, honey, it is so rough...... they even move the train station, it is so rough. People have done everything to get your pocketbook. I used to work in Buckhead where people wouldn't have to be scared. Around Mitchell Street, people were scared to get off the train they was so much going on. When people jumped off that train they were scared. They were tremblin'. That company was smart to move that train station from the back of Davidson's [department store]. They done move the bus station and I said 'thank you Jesus!' I didn't mind getting out in Buckhead at two o'clock in the morning, but nary a one gonna get off on Mitchell Street. People just be a hollerin' and they's more going on. Them colored people at that place was carryin' all kindsa weapons: knives, guns, blackjacks! They see they pocketbook and the women throw 'em down and run. They kill you on the spot with they switchblade knives. Sometimes they see a man and still catch him and kill him and say they didn't give them enough money!"

In the same tape, Louise discussed my mother's attitudes toward Jehovah's Witnesses. She would say that while I was off at college, at various times during the year, Jehovah's Witnesses would come around the neighborhood trying to spread their religion. She would say, "Ms. Sherer said not to let them in the house" and that "she didn't want any other nation trying to spread they religion."

This led to a discussion between me and Louise about how one knows when God calls you to preach. So I asked her that question. I asked her when it started with her, and she said it commenced when she was a younger woman. She said the Spirit would call out to her really loud and that for many years the Spirit called her but she didn't understand what was going on. She said she was "called to be a minister by the Spirit" while she was praying. She had some strong opinions about the distinction between what a minister was and a prophet was. She even said that her first husband, Willie, was a minister, that he was called from God, but he never made anything of himself because he wouldn't work. She also expressed strong opinions about people who call themselves ministers but were really false ministers. She said they could be rich and wear diamond rings and drive expensive cars, but they eventually go to hell because they're false ministers and false preachers. I then asked her what was a prophet was, and she answered that a prophet was a person who could tell you about the past, present, and future. Louise claimed that she was a prophet herself. False prophets, however, were people who were "in it just for the money." She then said that a prophet usually is not a minister and that many had been called to preach but only a few God has chosen to become both prophets and ministers.

She recounted to me how my younger brother, Daniel, had come down to her room one afternoon saying to her out of the blue, "Louise, you are a holy woman." She responded, "Daniel, I'm glad you see this in me." She goes on: "Daniel ain't no fool. He says to me, '365 days in a year I could talk to you bad and you still treat me good.'" She then told me how badly my mother was treating Daniel while I was away at college. She said my mother was "handing him some shit" and had been "treating him like a dog" and "runnin' him 'round like ragdoll." "'It's been that bad,' Daniel said. I'm tired of you talking to me that way.'" Louise laughs. "Oh

My brother Daniel and Louise share a beautiful moment.

your brother, Daniel, been suffering since you been gone off to college, David. Yo' momma really been rippin' his ass up. He go around the house going 'hee - hee, haw - haw - haw! When is my brother comin' home from college?'" "Well," I said, "I'm sorry he's having so much trouble. What do you think is wrong with Mom?" And Louise responded, "You know yo' momma is crazy. All of them Jewish womens loves to fuss. She jus' so damn hard on him all the time. Especially before she go oversea."

Louise was proud that Daniel said, "I don't care how mean I talk to you, you're always nice to me and you're a good, holy woman." Louise continues: "He even told the schoolteacher that." She said that Daniel said he had the "best maid in the world." She told me it made her feel good to hear that. She told him to just "have a nice day and you sure are a handsome boy." "Daniel been cryin' this whole year," she said. She added that she was afraid that Danny was on the "voige of a nervous breakdown." "Yo' momma has been treating him like a dog and your momma don't give a DAMN about him. 'I want David,' he would say. 'When my brother comin' back from college?' Yo momma really been tearin' his ass UP!"

###

My studies with Mr. Chanaka in DC had paid off in junior year at Emory when I declared music as my major with a concentration in piano. I fulfilled my pre-med requirements and applied for early decision to Boston University School of Medicine, where my father had gone before me. Despite rather mediocre MCAT scores, I made early decision due to my 3.74 GPA, solid interview, and, I have no doubt, the fact that I was a "legacy" student. Another factor was vital as well. At that time in the history of the admission process to medical schools in the United States, there was a shift away from favoring science majors to more closely considering students who were "well-rounded," candidates who had majored in history, political science, the arts, and the humanities. In contrast to the predictable chemistry, physics, or biology majors who, to most medical school admission committees, were as common as zealots in Jerusalem, these "well-rounded" students were a welcome change. In my year alone, Emory sent eight of us music majors on to medical school.

Despite my successes in college, I dreaded the rigors of medical school and wondered how I would be able to get through the first semester. Luckily, that year, 1979, Boston University School of Medicine was offering for the first time in its history the option of decompressing the first year of medical school into two years. (They even did a magazine article on me in their alumni magazine, complete with a photo portrait of me, so contemplative and actually quite depressed, at the piano.) Why they introduced this program eludes me, but I jumped at the chance. By taking a reduced workload, my self-doubt about my ability to complete the work was assuaged. Toe in the water and all that ~ my usual pattern. Unfortunately, my continuing lack of confidence was to dog me for years.

Then, in 1981, while Daniel was in his senior year at Whitman High School and during my sophomore year of medical school, the ax fell. A call to me in Boston from Danny shocked me. "Looks like Weezy is gone for good," he said. "Mom told the cops she stole some things and she's not here anymore. The Montgomery County police took her away!" I was struggling through school in Boston and since I no longer lived at the family homestead in Bethesda and had lost touch with events as they happened there, this news hit me like a mortal wound. Had I known back then that there was the very real chance that I would never see Weezy again ~ never have the chance to say goodbye, never hear her sing her gospel songs or utter her wonderful malapropisms, never again taste her fried chicken or bury my head in her fresh, menthol-scented neck ~ I would have caught the first plane out of Boston, rushed home, and gotten to the bottom of this impossible event.

Sure, she and Mom had had their share of fights over the years, often resulting in either Weezy quitting or getting fired, but none of those incidents had lasted more than a few days. The two proud, strong-willed women had always reconciled. This time, however, there would be no apologies or welcome-back hugs. Weezy was gone, and, heartless as it may sound, my anger and sense of injustice was such that I'd rather have learned that she was back in her first floor bedroom and had fired and permanently kicked out Mom.

In truth, Louise possessed something that neither of my parents could claim. With her warmth, her earthiness, her homespun wit and wisdom, and her unfailing belief in me, she, more than anyone else, had made me what I strove to become: a husband, father, professional, and, above all, what we Jews call a *mensch*: a person mature enough to do the right thing as often as humanly possible; a person who would not put himself first but would, like Louise, make difficult sacrifices for the welfare of others; a person brave enough to see the suffering in the lemon that is life and squeeze as much lemonade out as the fruit will allow.

Unfortunately, however, I did not go home when Danny phoned me back in 1981. Nor, up until 2011, did I ever try to locate Louise. Excuses now are easy: I had an education to complete, a profession to build, a life mate to find, and, later, a child to raise. There was no Internet to search, no cell phone records to scour, no Facebook to check. I have spent a good part of the last thirty years regretting this. But in my fifty-fifth year, I finally set out in earnest to find Louise Johnson Morris who would have been more than ninety years old by then. I had to know if she was alive. I needed to thank her for her incalculable gifts to my siblings and me. I was haunted that a debt needed to be repaid. Nothing, I thought, could even begin to sufficiently compensate Louise short of telling her how much it meant that she had helped me grow up functional in the neurotic, unhappy household in which I found myself as a child.

On summer break from med school and at home in Bethesda, I made numerous attempts to find out what really happened with Louise but to no avail. My mom stuck to the story Daniel had given, my father was mum, and my sisters were of no help. Even Danny, then on summer break from high school, could only repeat the version he gave me over the phone. I had no address or phone number for Louise or Chester. All leads were cold. Although stung by Louise's departure and powerless to do anything to find her, I wishfully believed that it was only temporary. My attentions turned elsewhere.

Like many young men, my most pressing issues at that time were making money and getting laid. I had an inside track on the first issue. I was able to secure employment at Washington Beef, which was family-owned and run by my friend Michael's father, Irvin, and his brothers. Washington

Beef was a meat-packing, shipping, and supplying business that served most of the upper-echelon restaurants in the Washington area. I was able to get a job there and, for the not-insignificant sum of five dollars an hour in 1981, spent a most of the summer in the frigid temperatures of their inner city plant. My day would start at about 5:30 a.m. when I would arrive to pick up my apron. When I first asked the foreman where I could get my smock, he stuck a stubby thumb in the air toward a stout, gnarled woman sitting in a small wire-encased enclosure and said, "Go see that bitch in the cage." I worked the line, hauling tenderloins, top rounds, chuck, and sirloins until my white-gloved hands were soaked with blood. By 9:30 each day it was lunch time, which either consisted of either a cinnamon roll and hot coffee from the roach coach, or, if I was feeling flush, a sit-down meal of scrambled eggs, bacon, and rye toast. Let me tell you; I felt like a real workin' man!

Washington Beef employed some of the rougher characters you could find in DC at that time: a mixture of blacks and lower- to lower-middle class whites worked the line. After a few days working the plant, I learned the nick - names for the restaurants Washington Beef supplied. Le Lion D'or became Lillian the Whore, the Jockey Club was the Jockey Strap Club, and Blackie's House of Beef was Blackie's Beat My Meat. There was this machine, the Cryovac machine, which was able to shrink-wrap food ~ beef, poultry, and lamb ~ airtight for freshness. The machine had a metallic, thumping beat to it, and the rhythm became so intoxicating that I devised a dance I taught the African American workers to perform to break the monotony of work.

The second issue that summer was coming along as well. I had the good fortune that a friend of Deb's was having a sleepover with Deb at my parents' house. She's a fairly well-known author now, but at the time I was physically a man (but emotionally about twelve) and she was an attractive woman my sister's age. I can remember sleeping in the room adjacent to my parents' one night when in she came in her nightgown and announced to me that Deb told her that I needed somebody to sleep with. Without missing a beat, I raised my eyes toward heaven, thanked Deb, and lifted up the blanket to let her in. Years later, I contacted the same woman and asked if she remembered Louise. With an enthusiastic yes, she recalled how she once saw Louise with a quarter taped to her forehead. Asking why, Louise responded, "We all needs money to live."

I, of course, woke up late the next morning and rushed off to Washington Beef, debating in the car over what excuse I might use for being late. Getting to work, the boys on the line asked me about my tardiness, and I told them that I had had a flat tire on the way to work. I thought it had made a pretty decent excuse, with sufficient theatrics, but each of them told me that that was "the oldest one in the book" and certainly I could come up with something much better than that.

There was no way I could know that, just six months before, in 1980, Louise was developing and expressing some attitudes toward my parents the significance of which I would not fully appreciate until decades later. In a particularly poignant exchange recorded on tape in December of 1980, Louise and Daniel discuss some issues that have made me rethink why Louise really left the family. Incredibly, Louise was under the impression that my parents were trying to kill her with witchcraft, and she spoke with Daniel how my father went to pay someone to put a spell on her. Louise goes on a long tirade about how she had treated the family over the course of two decades so well, raising the children, cooking food for the family, keeping the house neat and clean, taking care of Safta, and doing the job that "the mother" should be doing. In some very long exchanges on the tape, Daniel tries to get to the bottom of why my father hired someone to put a spell on her. Weezy doesn't give specific answers to that question, but in the tape she sounds totally convinced that both my parents were in on it. Daniel asked her exactly when the spell had been placed, and she said it had done last week. She said that the family had never bothered her to this extent before, but because of this spell, and what "colored people called being a snake in the grass," she felt it was getting close to the time that she had to leave.

She says to Daniel that "he ain't nobody's fool." "They did it. Not tried to do it but did it. They better get themselves another maid," she says. "You don't treat a member of the family like that." She then says that my dad didn't put a spell on her, but he was the one who paid for it. "After I raised you all I didn't think your parents would do that to me. I won't go along with that. I used to tell them they look good to me, but now they look like shit on a stick." She tells Daniel, "They made one mistake, I'm going to tell David about what they did to me." She relates how what they did to her was inexcusable on a "poor maid." She goes on to say how the witchcraft put her in a mess and she couldn't teach and preach to four thousand people anymore. She thought the spell was going to "tie" her. After she raised a

93

family from babies and endured such a long sacrifice, she felt that she couldn't be replaced. She goes on to say that she wasn't the best person in the world but that "God gave the family a blessing and then they run her away." She expresses to Daniel her wish that she could have had a maid when she was a young child. "Someone to care 'bout the kids and take care of the family." She felt that my mother Leah was crazy and guilty because she never made herself a mother to her children. She says to Daniel, "Ask David and Lisa about that." Louise then recounts how she thought that my mother did things only for herself. Daniel agrees. She said if it wasn't for her [Louise] feeding us, all of us kids would've grown up half-fed.

Now Louise was standing up for herself. "I gave them everything and took care of they babies." She said she used to have respect for my father, but "no mo.'" "Now it was my turn to turn my nose up to yo' momma. You don't want to fight the friend who took care of your children." Daniel asked for more, specifically about the spell, and Louise says, "You can eat it; you can drink it in water; you can spread it around." Daniel asks her if she's going to leave the family. She replies that they are "like dirty snakes and they don't deserve no maid like me."

Importantly, the tape reveals much about Louise's sensitivity and character. Hearing it for the first time in 2011, I had no idea of the resentment and bitterness that had built up inside of her. She knew that the children loved and revered her, and that, at one time, there was a connection between her and my parents. I was not aware, however, of the psychological or even psychiatric causes of her beliefs that my father had hired someone to use witchcraft on her and cast some sort of spell. Whether all of this was a descent into some form of mental illness or mere folklore belief, I suppose I will never know.

Listening to this first tape, I can see why my self-esteem and confidence as an adult had suffered. It seems that I found unending support and love from Louise while getting negative and critical messages from my mother. The constant tension that led me to believe that I would lose the most supportive person in my life must have led me to be constantly on edge about whether my main source of support, namely Louise, would be around or whether my mother would eventually force her from the home. Time and time again, I can see how Louise's general goodness, sweetness, and sheer humanity contrasted so starkly with my mother's desire for status, wealth, and recognition.

Strangely, a comical and light-hearted audio-tape is made a mere five months before the above session and is orchestrated by Daniel. In attendance are my father, Max, Daniel's good friend, Mark and Daniel. Louise happily participates in this farcical set-up later known as the "Mobutu Tape." It took place on April 20, 1980. Home from medical school on spring break, I participate as an actor as well. My father acts as photographer. We dress up in costumes: Louise dons a silk top hat and cape, I dress like some kind of quasi-Russian diplomat (with fur hat and heavy jacket), and Daniel is dressed as an Arab complete with long robes and a headdress. We employ one of my father's meerschaum pipes from London as an accessory. Our cat, Piewacket, is meandering in and out of the room. The absurdist, almost Dada-ist scene unfolds:

Louise enters the room and, given the meerschaum pipe to enjoy, sits in the "Central Chair of Honor." Daniel and Mark say, "Hi, Weezy!" She says, "What shall I do?" "Did you cook your chicken wings, Weezy?" the boys ask. "Good gracious alive!" she says in her wonderful, throaty laugh and goes on about "all that stuff on ~ different coats and hats and things; look at that stuff! Look at that cat! God, he's funny! We goin' to do what we did last time?" Louise, laughing heartily, can't get over the commotion: "They's more goin' on here..." Noticing the cat again she opines: "Them cats like all this love and stuff!"

Daniel cries: "Oh ~ Great ~Wee!" He then nonsensically introduces me as the leader of the Baha'i faith (he used to call me "the Ba'ab," the real founder of that religion) and with Louise sitting down in the Seat of Honor, Daniel, Mark, and I surround her in our costumes. Louise puts the meerschaum pipe in her mouth and places the "Mobutu" top hat on her head. Daniel mumbles something incongruously about the "Greek Autocephalous Church." Louise says, "This is a great costume." Danny remarks, "That ain't no costume, Wee, that's an o-fishul uny-form!" I blurt, "This is better than the Addams family." My father, laughing, butts in, "This IS the Addams family." Ending, we sign a fake proclamation as Daniel declares that this is going to conclude a "Triple Entente" between all the signatories (despite the fact that there are four of us signatories present.) Louise then states that Daniel looks like an a-rab, saying about his get-up, "It looks good on you." After the signing of the proclamation and the photography by my father to record the historic meeting, Daniel says we're to repair for dinner in the Grand Ballroom (Louise's chicken wings.) Daniel and I discuss the possibility that there may be an attempt on Louise's life. Louise asks, "Where do all this stuff come from ~ overseas? Good gracious alive!"

###

At the same time Weezy is expressing her attitudes to Daniel on tape about my parents, another tumult is brewing: Lisa's declining health.

Deb and I were invited to a New Year's Eve party at the parents of a friend of mine from high school. My parents were out. Daniel was out with friends. Lisa had just received a kidney transplant a few weeks before and was almost blind. Her nervous system had been ravaged by the juvenile diabetes she has suffered from for decades. She was left all alone in the house, not strong enough to get up and with no place to go. I debated whether I should go to the party with all the other revelers and try to have a good time on what usually is a festive occasion or stay with Lisa. I went to her room and saw her lying in bed. I saw her arm that used to have the functioning fistula in it for dialysis. I saw the color of her skin, which was so sallow and lacking in richness that anyone could plainly see she was severely ill. As she opened her eyes, she knew it was me, but she said she couldn't make out the details of my face. I told her that Deb and I were planning on going to a party but asked if she wanted me to stay with her instead. She told me to go ahead and have a good time, but there were such great sadness and resignation in her voice that I had to think carefully before I left. I felt her matted and coarse hair. Leaning over her, tears welled up in my eyes and fell thick and heavy on her face like the start of a spring rain. I think that was one of the most horrible and painful few minutes I ever spent on this Earth. I had a decision to make. I had been quite upset myself at that time, something about school ~ something about a girl ~ I don't remember which. I felt Deb and I both needed to get away and go to the party. Besides, I had met a girl the year before, the woman who would eventually become my wife, and I was hoping to see her again. After spending some time with Lisa, I told her that after the party I would come home and spend more time with her. I asked her if there is anything I could get her. She said "No, Mister," the pet name she had for me, and I again stroked her curly hair that had receded quite a bit because of the immune system-suppressing drugs she had taken. I told her that I would only go for a while and be back to spend time with her. She nodded her assent and fell asleep. Deb and I went off to the party.

Lisa's illness worsened over the course of the next few years to the point where, every few months, she'd threaten to stop her insulin therapy and in essence take her own life. I took her seriously and respected her courage to attempt to master her own fate. I never once judged her for I did not live a life like hers, full of doctor visits, painful interventions, and overall misery. I never really thought she would go through with it. Like the boy who cried "wolf," she had played that hand too many times. But on Sunday, December 5th, 1982, she called me while I was in Boston to say goodbye. "I've had too much of this, Mister," she said. Frustrated, I consoled her in the usual way whenever she would bring this up and tried to give her hope.

Then, on Wednesday, December 8th, Daniel called me. With tears and a shaking voice, he told me Lisa was dead. She had gotten an attorney to draw up papers stating that she did not want further treatment and, stopping her insulin on Monday, December 6th, slipped into a coma and fell on her sword in her own two-decade war with juvenile diabetes.

With a numb and unreal sense of finality, I told Daniel I would get the next available plane home to Washington.

At her funeral, I felt an enormous weight had been lifted from her and me. The crushing, unrelenting burden of such suffering was suddenly gone. She had been dealt a cruel and terrible set of cards and played it as best she could. There was nothing else left to do but grieve and remember.

I finished medical school in Boston in 1984, and, not sure of which direction to take, accepted a typically forgettable and painful internship year in internal medicine in Baltimore. I chose Baltimore because I wanted to be far enough from my parents and close enough to my girlfriend, Laura, who lived in DC, to strike a balance in work and life during what every new med school grad knows is an awful year. I tried my best to hide my most privy beliefs: "I'm a coward. I don't have the guts to quit my internship and throw in the doctoring towel." I began seeing a therapist who advised me to at least get my medical license by finishing my internship and taking Part III of my medical boards. It was sound advice. But the specter of my dead sister and images of her horrible, long-lasting demise exacted a price during that year. Her experiences colored my view of illness and medicine. I found it all so depressing. I felt I wasn't made of stern enough stuff to make a life out of this. Through this somewhat distorted lens, made worse by my sleep deprivation and own endogenous depression and anxiety, I made it to June 30th, 1985 where I decided I would take a break to travel, read, and look for options other than practicing medicine.

But options? I found few. I had been a student all my life, was egregiously naïve about "the real world," and, like most cowards, gave up too easily and too soon to make a profound change. Running short on money, I begrudgingly worked in a few clinics, took six months traveling and researching my first book on patient safety, and finally decided upon a residency in anesthesiology, where a spot had opened up at the University of Miami-Jackson Memorial Hospital program.

Why anesthesiology? Many of my internship colleagues had chosen the specialty in 1984. It simply was the "hot field" of the day. Traditionally, the weak sister of medical specialties and populated, at the time, mostly by doctors of foreign origin, anesthesiology had suddenly become the "it" girl. That it required no upfront expenses like establishing an office, building a practice, and maintaining a staff appealed to the "quicker exit" strategist in me. Toe in the water.

I actually enjoyed the succeeding three years in Miami: the weather, the comradeship with my fellow residents, the new skills to learn and master, and the vibrancy of the city were a boost to my confidence. I quickly made friends, many who owned boats, and there were parties everywhere. It didn't hurt that we residents in anesthesia, unlike in Baltimore, had the day off after call and that the place was a golfer's paradise. This was the time in Miami when the original television show *Miami Vice* was produced and filmed with Don Johnson as the sexy, pastel-bedecked Sonny Crockett. I even saw them filming near my South Beach apartment on the 16th floor on Belle Isle, overlooking the ocean and inland waterway. The town's trademarks were: cigarette boats, flashy cars, drugs, sex and transience.

###

After finishing residency in Miami in 1989, I headed back to Bethesda for my first real job out of training. It was a backsliding disaster. Numerous pressures exerted their weight ~ a new (and wrong) stressful job with incredibly demanding hours, lack of full confidence in my skills, finding the right place to live, and whether to get married to my longtime girlfriend, Laura. It was the start of summer, the times in my Somerset-fixated mindset associated with easy living, vacations, and endless days in the sun. All that I could think of was that although I was finally a doctor, a professional, with real responsibilities and a reputation to build and maintain, deep down I really wanted none of it. Truthfully, I was really still a child: insecure, overly nostalgic, fearful, resentful of pressures that my parents had placed on me to become a physician. That I had finally arrived at this point of unhappiness, misery, and a career completely lacking in creativity or artistic relevance left me bitter. I failed miserably in what 1 Corinthians 13:11 states: "When I was a child, I spake as a child, I understood as a child, I thought as a child: but when I became a man, I put away childish things."

That, I seemed unable to do.

I was jealous of my art historian brother who was getting his Ph.D. in art history at Harvard and my artist sister who was living in Israel, throwing pots in art school, and doing hash in what I perceived as an exotic and bohemian life. I felt stifled, disenchanted, and pegged into a career I did not want. I felt like a prisoner. All this work was for naught. It wasn't for me.

I lasted at that job for three months and spent the next three years bouncing around various jobs in Florida, trying to buy time and salvage the situation, until I landed a more palatable position, lifestyle-wise at least, in the DC suburbs. I was able to maintain a few jobs like that, with no on-call and no weekends, for twenty years, during which time I bought my first house, married Laura, got a dog, and, after seven years of marriage, had the courage to have a child. My struggles with depression and anxiety continued intermittently through those decades, and, like most sufferers with some degree of insight, I knew that both genetics and upbringing were my enemies. I have no doubts, however, that Louise's influence upon me, so different from my parents', saved my life. Her unconditional love, humor, and wisdom infused me with enough positive energy to allow me to dodge the usual scourges of drug abuse, alcohol abuse, eating disorders, tumultuous interpersonal relationships, or blind desire for money or status that is so common in people in my demographic. There can be no recompense adequate for that.

In 2011, at age fifty-four and after almost half my adult life working as an anesthesiologist in the hamster-wheel that is life in the DC metro area, a variety of factors led me into a depression whose soil was so deep you could have sown coconuts into the grooves. The usual suspects of that age were there: work stress, family responsibilities, concerns about my own health, and the classic question of whether the grind we urbanites find ourselves in is worth all the damn trouble. Heeding the wisdom of Thoreau, I reflected on his words: "Most men lead lives of quiet desperation and go to the grave with the song still in them." The time was ripe for me to "take stock" of myself. Not being much of a man for material things (no country clubs, I keep cars ten years on average, $15 is enough for a bottle of red, I live within my means), I was fortunate that I had just enough time, desire, and insight to reflect. That meant tying up some loose ends -- the loosest of which was: "What happened to Louise?"

Chapter Seven

From House to House

ಬಿಂ

Weezy: The Missing Years
1947-1959

Once I had decided in earnest to try and find out if Louise was still alive, I took all the materials and resources available to me in 2011, did some detective work, and tried to sketch out her past. Perhaps the most valuable information about Louise's life after her divorce from her first husband, Felix Holloman, came from my brother's Archives. Rummaging through the various family documents, homemade works of art, "borrowed" library books, and long-playing records of Romanian folk music, I came across a mother lode of documents and tape recordings relating both to Louise and Chester. These include Chester's original birth certificate, some baby pictures, letters, health records, birth album, and, I am even ashamed to say, a small newborn's brass ring that was a gift of the Boykin's Jewelry Company in Mineral Wells, Texas in the days after Chester's birth.

How or why these things were left behind after Louise left our family's employ I don't know. Did she just plain forget them in the aftermath of the shock of being fired? Did she not know the documents were at our home? I know that Daniel would not have taken them from her and put them in the Archives while she was still living with us. Nevertheless, what I do know is that these recordings, papers, and images were of such value in reconstructing a life so difficult and nomadic that it would be impossible for me to tell this story without them.

Since Louise was born in 1922, I know she first married at the age of twenty-two because I obtained a copy from Bibb County, where Macon resides, of the general index of marriages. According to that record, her marriage to Felix Holloman took place August 19, 1944. Sadly, I have no record either from Louise herself, Chester, or Louise's family about the time she spent with Felix. She never talked about him or their time together.

The next useful piece of information I was able to garner is a most incredible document, the request for divorce dated April 9, 1947 from attorney R.L. Smith. The letter reads:

R.L. Smith, Attorney and Counselor at Law of general practice in all courts
226½ Cotton Ave.
Macon, GA
April 9, 1947

Mrs. Louise J. Johnson Holloman, 2130 N. Howard St., Baltimore, MD
Your husband, Felix Holloman, has engaged me to file suit for divorce from you, and, as I understand, you also

would be glad to be given a divorce from him as you two could not get along together.

If you'll sign the inclosed (sic) sheet which I am sending to you on the line at the bottom where you see the check mark and return it to me in the inclosed (sic) stamped envelope, we will be able to have the divorce decree rendered at the June term, 1947, and you will not have to appear in court and will not have to pay any attorney fees for your divorce.

Thanking you in advance for this favor,

> I am, yours truly,
> R.L. Smith, attorney for Felix Holloman
> P.S.: The thin copy is for you to keep. RLS

This original divorce request is so telling for the time in its dismissive and condescending tone and lack of regard for the rights of women, especially black women. It speaks for itself.

The puzzle of Louise's past was missing a lot of pieces. Whether Louise and Felix had lived together in Baltimore or whether they had separated and Louise had moved on to Baltimore is something I've never been able to discern. I haven't the first clue what Louise was doing in Baltimore in 1947. However, this pattern of movement between the South and the North, from Texas to Georgia, the Carolinas, Baltimore, and Washington, DC was her M. O. in these missing years.

After her divorce from Felix, the next place I am able to definitively place Louise is in Mineral Wells, Texas after her marriage to Willie Morris. About him I also know very little, though there is more information than about Felix Holloman. Louise's family and Chester himself were unable to enlighten me about Willie and his relationship with Weezy. The best information emanates from what she herself told me when I was growing up and from a tape that my brother recorded sometime in the 1970s. What Weezy related to us as children was confirmed in the tape in which she speaks about her time with Willie in Texas and also how she discovered it was her calling to be a minister. She says: "The Spirit started talking really loud to me in Texas. It said to me, 'Louise, you're a reader.' This was about the time that white boy got killed after he was held for ransom. You know, Daniel, that boy named Bobby Greenlease. He was a white boy that they killed. Po' critter. That's when the Spirit started calling me real loud."

The white boy that Louise was referring to was the subject of perhaps the second most notorious childhood kidnapping and murder in United States history, the first being that of the "Lindbergh baby," the son of Charles Lindbergh. Bobby Greenlease was born in 1947 and was the son of a prominent car dealer, R.C. Greenlease, who had car dealerships all the way from Texas to the Dakotas. His son, Bobby, was kidnapped when he was six years old and killed by his abductors, two drug addicts and alcoholics, a man and woman, even after the ransom of $600,000 was paid. Until that time, that was the largest sum ever paid for ransom in the history of our country.

"Willie was very religious too," Louise says, "but he wouldn't work. He was a Called Minister of God. I had the Spirit called to me when I was prayin'. He told me people can go to Hell if they's false preachers. You know, Daniel, you seen them on TV wearing they diamond rings. You know like Reverend Ike. He ain't no minister. I'm both a prophet and minister. A prophet can tell the past, present, and future. But there are false prophets. They put God into something and hope that people will give you money. People can make like they are ministers, but usually a prophet is not a minister. Many have been called to preach, but a few God has chosen."

I do not have a definitive answer as to why Louise and Willie, a young married couple from Georgia, moved to a relatively remote town in Texas in the late 1940s, but I have an idea. It relates to what is a curious historical oddity called the Baker Hotel. Mineral Wells is a town that lies about forty miles west of Fort Worth and, today, is a community of about 18,000 people. In the late 1800s, mineral waters were found on a farm owned by a man named J.A. Lynch. There is a local legend that an epileptic woman, thought at the time to be crazy, drank the water and was cured of her illness (a latter day Pool of Bethesda, perhaps?) Word got around, and folks began digging wells left and right in the hopes of gaining access to these miraculous waters. The population exploded, and by the 1930s it had grown to almost 40,000.

To support the visitors that came from far and wide, hotels sprang up in the city. One of them was the Crazy Water Well and Hotel that took its name from the legend mentioned above. But the most well-known hotel of all was built by a man named T.B. Baker and was called the Baker Hotel. Opening in November 1929, it was the only skyscraper outside of a major metropolitan area in the United States. Photographer Rick Waldroup describes it this way: "The hotel was 14 stories high and had 450 rooms. It towered over everything in downtown Mineral Wells and could be seen for miles in any direction. The hotel had its own underground well and bathhouse, and it also housed the first swimming pool ever built for a hotel in Texas. The ballroom on the 12th floor was named the Cloud Room because of the painted clouds on the ceiling. It was always busy every weekend with one band or another and became the place to be. Indeed the Baker hotel became a national phenomenon, drawing visitors from all over, especially movie stars and celebrities. Some of the well-known celebrities to stay at the Baker included Gene Autry, Lucille Ball, Bonnie and Clyde, George H.W. Bush, Jack Dempsey, Clark Gable, Judy Garland, Jean Harlow, John F. Kennedy, Will Rogers... and many more."

I have no proof that Louise worked at the Baker Hotel or at any other hotel in Mineral Wells while she was there, but knowing her accounts of Willie's apparent allergy to work, it seems reasonable that she was the major financial support to the family. Since Mineral Wells thrived on being a tourist destination, it is not too much of a stretch to suggest that she either worked at the hotel or in some related service-oriented field as a maid, kitchen help, or nanny. Being young, black, female, and lacking in higher education, I figured that was about as well as you could do for those times in Texas.

In research conducted in 2013, I was heartened to learn that the distance between Louise's address in Mineral Wells on SE 7th Street and the Baker Hotel on East Hubbard was less than half a mile. In a town of over twenty square miles, the proximity of the two locales gave further credence to my theory that she was somehow connected to the hotel.

Daniel's Archive yielded much more. Chester's birth certificate revealed he was born not on July 29th, as Louise had always told me, but July 28, 1953 at Nazareth Hospital in Mineral Wells. The Nazareth Hospital has its own storied history, but simply put, it started as the Mineral Wells Clinic and was built soon after the Crazy Hotel opened in the late 1920s, which replaced the Crazy Flats Hotel that burned in the mid 1920s. In 1931, the Holy Sisters of the Nazareth bought the facility and made the top floor of the building their place to live and take care of patients. The hospital closed in the mid-1960s and moved briefly to the Crazy Hotel until the present hospital was built.

The baby book that Louise and Willie received from the Nazareth Hospital upon Chester's birth is an incredible piece of Texas history. It was presented with the salutation: "Congratulations! This book is presented to you by the progressive business concerns whose letters are part of this book. It is their way of expressing goodwill and friendship. A reply is enclosed for each business concern and they would appreciate knowing if you received it and also your opinion. They sincerely hope that you received it in the spirit in which it was presented."

Fully illustrated, bound, and quality-made, it was chock full of cordial greetings and discount certificates to local businesses, and it belied the widespread racism in the southern United States at the time.

A sampling of the advertisements reads: "Dear folks: a new baby usually means it's time to save a little extra money. This coupon will save you $50 on any new car or used 1949 model or later car or truck Van Natta–King Motor Co., Mineral Wells, Texas. No trade-ins. Only one coupon to apply named Louise Morris address 406 SE. 7th St., Mineral Wells, Texas."

And: "Congratulations! Please accept our gift of $10 discount on any washing machine or major appliance (void after six months), Massingale Appliance Company, Mineral Wells, Texas."

And: "Our congratulatory gift certificate good for one suit or dress cleaned and pressed. Just phone for our courteous route man or present the slip to Moulder Dry Cleaners, Mineral Wells, Texas."

Poring over this memorabilia got me wondering about the patient population of Nazareth Hospital at the time Chester was born. They had to be mostly minority or poor, I reasoned. Mostly black? Perhaps Latino? The kind sentiments expressed in the card that accompanied the book and the fact that the giving of such a gift to a poor black woman in 1953 in the South, albeit while shilling for local businesses, begs the question of whether blacks were treated differently in Texas than in more easterly southern states like Alabama, Mississippi, and Georgia. That it was a Catholic hospital makes we wonder if the attitudes at the time toward women like Louise were more liberal than in the Baptist hospitals of Dallas, Houston, or Galveston.

My gut tells me that much anti-black sentiment in the Deep South had traditionally gone hand in hand with anti-Semitism and anti-Catholicism. Indeed, a study of the history of the Ku Klux Klan and its offshoots (The Knights of the White Camellia, The Knights of the Golden Circle, etc.) reveals that the earlier iterations of these groups would never accept a Catholic into their ranks even though Catholics are, to many believers, the "original" Christians. This puzzled me as a kid for I saw the world, religiously at least, as being divided into three groups: Christian, Jew, and Other. Aside from their penchant for lynching, beating, and torturing blacks, tarring and feathering Jews, and otherwise hating anyone else not like them, the Klan treated Catholics with disdain at the very least and violence in the worst scenarios.

That opinion comes from a strongly personal incident in my own, distant past. As an eight year old, alone on a Friday night save for Danny asleep, Louise in her room, and

Freddie by my side, I watched in horror (on my parents' new RCA Victor color TV), snug in footy pajamas in my parents' bedroom, the 1963 film *The Cardinal* produced and directed by Otto Preminger. In the scene in question, a Catholic priest gets assaulted by the Klan after trying to help some poor black victims who got beaten by the racist group. A group of Klan thugs, about a dozen in all in white hoods and robes, grab the priest and rip open his clothes.

Klansman: "Hey, hey. What you call this thang (holding a crucifix)? I mean, the fancy name."

Priest: "A crucifix."

Klansman: "Yeah, that's what the nigger called it when I took it away from him. He was kinda queer for it. He wanted to kiss it while we were strengthening his character (the other Klansmen laugh.) We ain't gonna stand for that kinda stuff. Hey. You know what you're gonna have to do with this little old statue, Padre? You're gonna spit on it!"

Priest: "And what would that prove? Except that you've been able to scare one particular priest into defiling the image of Christ."

Klansman: "Well, maybe that's just plenty. You gonna go back home and tell them other nigger lovers up North that they ain't welcome down here! Now you spit on it!"

When the priest refuses, he holds the crucifix as the Klansman whips him with a bull whip, the others in the group clapping in time to their merrily sung rendition of "Dixie."

The scene scared the hell out of me. I thought of Louise in the basement, reading her Bible, alone on a Saturday night, her son way across town.

My supposition is that these common enemies to southern bigots may have created a sort of kinship between blacks and Catholics, and Louise's treatment at Nazareth Hospital may have been a reflection of that.

Louise's stay in Texas did not last long. By 1954, Chester's medical records and some postmarked envelopes show that Louise moved back to Georgia with Chester. Whether Willie went with them no one seems to know. Louise may have moved in with her sister, Susie Sublett, who lived at 240 North West Sunset Ave. in Atlanta. Incredibly, I later learned this was the same street where Martin Luther King, Jr. had lived. I have Chester's medical records from the Fulton County Medical Clinic from 1955, which was located at 186 NW Sunset Ave. in Atlanta. Louise, I surmised, stayed with her sister for a while until she got on her feet. Another envelope I found, addressed to Louise Morris, reveals the address 540 Hunter Ave. SW, Atlanta but was not postmarked.

Perhaps the best of the sparse evidence of Louise's life at that time came from a tape that I recorded in the summer of 1977 after my first year at Emory University in Atlanta. I was back at home in Bethesda and had a summer job working at Washington Beef. After having spent my first year away from home in the undisputed capital of the "New South", I was eager to hear what Louise could tell me about her experience with the city. What I got was Louise's description of what it was like in Atlanta after she had returned from Mineral Wells. She says: "I was working in Buckhead and had to catch the bus off Mitchell Street. It was so dangerous down there, David. Some of them Negroes ain't even graduated the seventh grade. They just common. Cussin', doing dope, and raisin' sand. Don't know where they next meal is common from. This is why I thank God for such a good mom and dad. I wasn't used to thangs bein' like this."

This tape, referenced earlier in this book, foreshadows the theme of Louise as protected minister of God in another of Daniel's recordings, when she took to the street preaching in DC a full decade later in the mid-1960s. In the that tape she tells me: "I preached on the corner of 12th and I Street. I'm not scared because God gave me that place ~ people don't even pay anyone no 'tension. I prayed in the church for God to give me a safe spot. They don't even touch me. If anyone threatens me I say, 'Man, put that knife back in your pocket.' People would protect me. They would say, 'That's a good woman.' That's the corner that God gave me. The right-hand side he give me but not the left-hand side. God, I want to be protected, and I want to be near my son. The police would tell me, 'It's against the law to play music. Preach all you want to.' They would say, 'Lady, you are doing a wonderful job helping with the bums and drunks.' They would ask me, 'What do you talk to them about?' I just talk to them about God. I have prayed there for many years and God always said he would protect me; he only give me the one side of the street. The police said you ain't supposed to go no further than what he gave you when you prayed."

Interestingly, in the same tape she picks up on her theme about Jehovah's Witnesses. She says: "My own momma didn't let the Jehovah's Witnesses in the house. Some of them be crooks ~ they would get the dope on the inside and tell it to the folks on the outside. We wouldn't let them in the house. When they would come around this house [meaning the Sherers'] I'd say, 'I'm just they maid and these folks is Jewish and they don't believe in it. Bye!' Is these people ministers? I say hell no! It ain't but three called ministers in

Washington and nary a one is a Jehovah's Witness. Some of these ministers go out and bet on the horses, so that ain't no minister. Even you've got more sense than that, David. Even a child like Daniel can tell that I'm a holy woman."

The trail, with many blanks in the interim, picks up again in Washington, DC with a treasure of documents that brings Louise closer to my family's orbit. By 1957, my birth year, Louise is now with Chester in Washington, DC. She is most likely separated or divorced from Willie because no further reference is made to him until 1966 when letters reveal that the thirteen-year-old Chester visited him in Spartanburg, South Carolina.

One other potential link to Willie (prior to the Spartanburg letters of 1966) is revealed in a single envelope addressed to Louise from Willie and Louise's last known address of 412 S. E. 7th St. in Mineral Wells, Texas dated December 14, 1957 addressed to Ms. Louise Morris care of May Mary McDade (who was, I later discovered, one of Louise's sisters), 646 Morton Pl. NE., Washington, DC. I doubt it was from Willie, though, because it appears to be in a woman's handwriting.

Immunization records, envelopes, and school records now place Louise and Chester at various locations in the nation's capital, and it was here that she would spend the next twenty-five years of her life, which included those life-changing years (for me) that I got to know her.

These records from the Nazareth Hospital, Fulton County Health Clinic, and later records from the District of Columbia Department of Public Health, the District of

David Sherer

Columbia Division of Surplus Food, Metropolitan DC Boys Club, and other public welfare programs were not only valuable in helping me trace Louise's whereabouts, they are historically important in that they reveal the natural extensions of the social safety net that came out of Roosevelt's four terms as president to help people in need make their way through life. This work was later carried on and expanded during President Johnson's Great Society and, along with the Civil Rights Act of 1964, was crucial to improving the lives of people like Louise and Chester.

Daniel's Archive is full of local examples of assistance that Louise received. For example, in order to apply for assistance from the Division of Surplus Food (also known as public assistance) located at 815 Rhode Island Ave. NW, Washington, DC, Louise had to prove that she had been a resident of the District of Columbia for at least one year. I have a note dated December 16, 1957 in which a representative of the Quaker City Life Insurance Company attests to the satisfaction of this requirement: "Sir: this is to state that I have known Mrs. Louise Morris to have lived in Washington, DC for at least one year. F. Bidle, Quaker City Life Insurance Company, 1416 I Street, Northwest DC."

Or this one: "Case number 89549. District of Columbia Health Department, Bureau of Maternal and Child Welfare; clinic number 5, appointment book, Chester Morris birthdate 7/28/53. Certificate of immunizations: 'This is to certify that Chester Lee Morris has completed a series of three injections for protective immunity against diphtheria whooping cough and tetanus on 11/22/55 at the age of one year (sic). Booster doses for diphtheria whooping cough and tetanus were given on 7/25/57. Vaccination against polio was given on 10/15/56, 12/27/56, 8/29/57. Vaccination against smallpox was successful on 5/14/54. Dated 1 30/58 signed M. Paul M.D. This certificate will be needed for school registration. Keep in a safe place with birth certificate ~ to be retained by parents.'"

The Archives also bear witness to my mother's helpfulness. For instance, once Louise secured employment with my family in 1959, Mom made sure Louise was able to navigate her way through DC and the Maryland suburbs and get her basic needs met. This was the liberal, full of life young mother I knew on Colston Drive in Silver Spring and Somerset on Essex Ave. Here is a sample, which was written in my mother's meticulous Spencerian cursive (honed and perfected at Philadelphia High School for Girls), directing Louise on what seems like a task out of the Labors of Hercules:

"1.   Board # 70 bus @ Georgia Ave.
 2.   Ride down to 7th and Florida
 3.   Board #90 bus marked 17th + Penna Ave., SE
 4.   Ride to New Jersey Ave + L Street
 5.   Walk ½ block to 3rd St."

Here's another for getting Chester into a different school and arranging housing: "Between 1 and 4 PM on Sept. 4th, Principal request transfer to Nolle School, at 50th + "C" St, SE. Also, speak to Mrs. Elizabeth Johnson, wife of Rev. M Johnson, phone LU41834, about Chester living place 4727 B St SE."

Mom, to her credit, also helped Louise get young Chester into summer camp with the Metropolitan Police Boys Club located in Scotland, Maryland. She filled out the forms, made sure Chester had all the correct articles (and they were many for a kid limited of means: bathing trunks, poncho or raincoat, pants, shirts, coat or sweater, socks, shoes, pajamas, handkerchiefs, towels, soap, toothbrush and toothpaste or powder, and suitcase), and was able to get him transported to the Boys Club departure and pick-up point at 1010 3rd St NW in DC.

In summers when Chester was not at camp and Louise could afford it, he was sent to South Carolina to visit his father. Some of the letters, also known as "the Spartanburg letters," sent home from that time are quite touching. (Please note misspellings and grammar were not changed.) They reference caretakers even Chester cannot recall today:

"Aug 10, 1966
332 Fowler St
Spartanburg, SC

Dear Mother,

How are you doing? I am doing fine. Think (sic) for letting me go on the trip. I'm enjoying myself very much. Willie and I go some place everyday. We do see a lot of Beautiful building down here. I so do miss seeing you. Mrs. Claude is a very nice person. I wish I could come down here more often. Hope you are well and not working to hard. We be home soon.

Love from your son."

And this letter from a caretaker:

"Dear Louise,

Just a few lines to let you hear from us. Everything here is OK.....(Willie) and Chester goes out almost every day. He is having a good time. Me, I have been a little sick going to the doctor Saturday. I brought Chester pills I make him take one every day. His nose have not bleed since we been here. He love my sister, like her cooking. Everyone here think he is a nice little boy. We go to the movies Thursday. We have plenty of things to eat. Don't worry about him, he is in good hands. If you want to write to him, write to:

Mr Chester Morris
332 Charles St
Spartanburg, SC

Ah Ah. Chester stayed wake all nite looking out the window. He was surprise to see so many large building here. Hope to be home soon. Willie write you let you know when he be leaving.

Mrs Erna Jones"

I was astounded to discover in 2013 that these letters from a son and caretaker to a distant and often absent mother were written within weeks of the very letters I and my sisters wrote to my parents as they were touring Europe and the Middle East in the summer of 1966.

###

Mom was so helpful to Louise in those early times, for Louise and Chester were like "wandering Jews" themselves. In the span of four years, Chester spent time not only at different schools but living at various DC addresses: Florida

Ave. between 5th and 6th; 646 Morton Pl., NE; 4727 B St. SE; 625 Dahlia St. NW.

The fact that Louise could only see him Thursday evenings and Saturday evening through Sunday forced me to reevaluate my own lot as I matured as an adult. Growing up in a home of relative abundance, I never felt the deprivation or was exposed to the hardships Chester and Louise surely endured. These precious scraps of paper, photographs, and tape recordings are all I have left to tell the struggle that Louise encountered before finally settling down to the twenty-two year working relationship with my family. That she finally found a place for steady employment, housing, and health care for herself and her son must have been a relief for the thirty-eight-year-old Louise, but being away from her son five out of seven days a week, and having her other son, Christopher, under adoption, was wrenching. My mother recalls Louise saying to Chester on the phone, "You is my heart. Don't forget to bresh yo' teeth." It was a sad reality ~ a situation that would exact a toll on any mother and child, particularly if you were short on money and black in a land where being white, Anglo-Saxon, and Protestant was considered the model of what it meant to be an American.

Chapter Eight

Close to Home

ೞೂೞ

Chester and Discovery
December 2011

By the fall of 2011, it had become apparent that the only realistic way I was going to learn Louise's fate was to find the only other potentially living link I had ~ her son, Chester. In my life, the only other person related to Louise by blood that I had ever spoken to was her sister, Susie Sublett, who lived on Sunset Avenue in Atlanta. I can remember one of my first acts upon settling into my apartment in the fall of 1976 across the street from the Emory Law School was to call Susie and introduce myself. Her husband, Emmanuel, answered the phone. "Excuse me," he said. "I have peanut in my mouf'. Who did you say you was?" I chatted with Susie off and on that fall, giving her regards from her sister up North. I later learned she had died in 2011 at age 101.

It was inescapable that Chester, if he himself were alive, would be my best bet in finding Louise. I had last spoken to Chester perhaps forty years earlier when I was fourteen years old. We never had a close relationship, but we had seen each other perhaps once or twice a year from the mid-1960s to the early 1970s. As mentioned previously, he went by the name Pete, but I figured whatever search I conducted, my best bet was to use his full legal name: Chester Lee Morris. Standard Google and other search engine research produced nothing of value. After weeks of dead ends, one public records source, Intelius, turned up something promising. A Chester Lee Morris, whose present address was in Gwynn Oak, Maryland, had as a prior address on Sunset Avenue in Atlanta. My heart skipped a beat. Pay dirt! I knew this was my man. Find him, and I could find Louise.

Excitedly, I called the numbers associated with that address. No answers ~ not even a message machine or voice mail. Disappointed and frustrated, I figured I'd come to another dead end. But I had an idea. My niece, Mia, and her husband, Jorge, were living in Baltimore. I called Mia and suggested I invite myself up for lunch Sunday, December 5th, 2011 with the hopes of driving to Chester's last known address. Mia had been following my attempts to write about Louise, so she happily agreed.

That Saturday morning over coffee, cheese, and bread, Mia and Jorge questioned me about my thoughts and feelings. Was I scared? Excited? What would I say if Chester was home? Did I think he'd be angry? Bitter? Jazzed at my own curiosity, courage, and perseverance, I wasn't quite sure what I was feeling or how I would react if Pete was really home that day.

Having done my medical internship at Sinai Hospital of Baltimore in 1984, I had known the city fairly well.

Gwynn Oak was another matter. With my MapQuest-generated guide sitting on the seat next to me, I negotiated my way through some of Baltimore's worst neighborhoods. Driving along the main road that eventually connected to I-695, Baltimore's Beltway, I took a turn only to find I was heading the wrong way. I got even more lost, pushed the car to the side of the road, and asked two middle-aged black ladies where such and such a road was. I called them both "ma'am," asking them for directions. Initial expressions of puzzlement and a touch of wariness gave way to smiles on their faces. After thanking them politely for their help, one turned to me and said, "No problem, baby." I thanked them again and told him to have a "blessed day," figuring they were churchgoers. I was repaid with broad smiles.

As I closed in on Chester's address, the neighborhoods began to improve. Broken-down brownstones gave way to cleaner condos and those in turn yielded to middle-class, single-family homes on clean, tree-lined streets. After finding Chester's address, I parked the car, took a deep breath, and knocked on the door. A dog's bark leapt from the house. After a minute or so of no answer, I rang the bell again. Again another bark. No answer.

Disappointed, I figured either Chester was not home or worse, no longer lived there. I looked in the mailbox and saw mail addressed to a Vernon Smith. I had learned from my Intelius search that there were people in Chester's household that bore the last name of Smith but no Vernon that I had recalled.

Dejected, I took some scrap paper from my pocket. On it I wrote: "I am looking for a man named Chester Lee Morris. I don't know if he still lives here. My name is Dr. David

Sherer. Would you be kind enough to forward this phone number to him, if possible? Thank you. D J Sherer M.D.

P.S. I knew him and his mother many years ago."

Downcast, I returned to the car and headed back to DC. "So much for that," I figured. My chances of finding Louise, I thought, were next to nil.

That evening at about 5:00 the phone at my home rang. I was fiddling around on Facebook and my son, Liam, answered. "Daniel Sherer? He doesn't live here," Liam said. I glanced over at him, figuring it was a mistaken call for my brother, and my first instinct was to tell Liam to just tell the caller he had the wrong number. But then something deep in my cortex told me to answer that call. I went over and took up the receiver.

"Hello," the voice said, "David, this is Chester." I broke out into a big smile. I said, "How are you? I've been searching for you for months!' This was a voice that I hadn't heard in over forty years! After small talk, I broached the crucial question: Is your mother alive? "Why yes!" he said, "She's going to be ninety in March. She lives in Macon." I was overjoyed. My mind raced ahead to when I could see her. "Is she well? Is her mind still there?" I asked. Chester explained that she was wheelchair-bound, in and out of lucidity, and required constant nursing care. It was hard for me to grasp. "I'd like to see you, Chester," I said. "Any chance we could have dinner together? I could come to Baltimore and take you and your family to dinner at the Inner Harbor to catch up on old times." We set the date for mid-December. I was stunned by my good fortune.

On Sunday evening, December 8th, 2011, I met Chester, his wife, and their seventeen-year-old son JaQuan at Phillips Seafood at the Inner Harbor. It wasn't hard to recognize

Chester ~ he's six foot seven. His son is even taller. I stared into the face I hadn't seen in four decades and eerily saw his mother looking back at me. After an awkward hug, he introduced me to his family. At dinner, he told me how he had spent the intervening years ~ how Louise came to live with him after she left my parents' employ and how she left because my parents wouldn't give her a raise. He talked about his years living under various caretakers, his struggles, his accomplishment of getting a college degree at Bowie State University, and his starting and raising a family.

I was fixated on Louise's fate after 1981. She lived with him at 12th and H St. NW, Washington, DC, moved briefly on to Atlanta, and then finally to Macon, her birthplace, where most of her remaining family lived at a compound known as the "Home-House," close to the original Johnson Farm. He showed me some pictures of Louise, and I was shocked at the toll time had taken on her. The robust, strong, beautiful woman I had known for the twenty most formative years of my life was now debilitated, gray, and frail.

During dinner, I handed Chester the Spartanburg letters he had written to his mother in 1966 when he was staying with a caretaker in South Carolina. I had saved them all these years with the hope that someday I could return them to him. His wife began to read them and started to cry. Finally I asked if he thought Louise would know me if I visited her. He said he couldn't be sure. "Would it be acceptable to you if I went to see her? I'd love to see her before it's too late. I'm trying to write a book honoring her life and our relationship." He said that that would be fine with him, and he would put me in touch with his cousin, Diane, who visited Louise frequently at the nursing home. I was overjoyed.

We parted telling each other that we would keep in touch. Armed with Diane's phone number, I strode back to my car, incredulous that a void of over three decades was about to be filled.

The next day I called Diane. She said she had already spoken to Chester and knew the purpose of my call. She could not have been nicer. After telling her about my relationship with "Aunt Louise," I asked when the best time for a visit was. "Most any weekend," she said. I found that my first opportunity to schedule a visit was the Martin Luther King, Jr. holiday weekend in January. She confirmed that that would work for her. The phone was still warm in the receiver as I was at the computer booking my flight to Atlanta. "Hang on, Weezy!" I thought. "I'm coming to see you!" The gospel tune Louise sang almost daily, whenever she was in "high spirit," made its way into my head: "I be shouting, come the judgment day!"

Chapter Nine

On the Road to the "Home-House"

ဆာလ

Macon, Georgia
January 15, 2012

This was the day for which I had waited thirty-one years, the day I thought would never come. I had arrived in Atlanta on a Saturday, the morning before, and stayed overnight at my former professor and friend's house near the Emory University campus. Dr. Tom Flynn, Professor of Philosophy at Emory University, had kindly agreed to put me up over the Martin Luther King, Jr. holiday weekend. The irony of that weekend's historical significance was not lost on me, nor was the fact that the previous year, when I started my search in earnest for Louise, marked the 150th anniversary of the start of the Civil War.

Growing up, I had heard so much about Macon from Louise. The day was bright and the traffic minimal, and as I drove the 80-plus miles south from Atlanta to Macon on

I-85 images of the city I had never seen made their way into my consciousness. I imagined the farm she had grown up on with her six sisters and three brothers. I pictured her pushing the plow hitched to the mule.

I turned on the radio to keep my mind off the impending emotional thunderstorm that I knew was coming. Satellite radio kept me occupied. A leftist professor from the University of Massachusetts at Amherst, Richard Wolff, was being interviewed about the "Occupy" movements that had swept across the United States in 2011. On another channel, Gordon Adams, a defense expert, was opining on the present defense positions of the United States and which nations or groups posed the most likely threat to democracy in the coming decades.

I firmly believe in the "mind's eye" and often was the time that Louise had told me that there "is such as this." Before my journey, I had used MapQuest to locate the nursing home that Louise lived in on Anthony Street and saw that upon exiting I-85, one took a right-hand turn, a left, and then a right up the hill. The plans were to meet Louise's niece, Diane, at 2:00 p.m. that day at the Heritage Healthcare nursing home, but because the weather was clear and there was sparse traffic, I arrived just after 1:00 p.m. The facilities sat nestled on top of the hill on the right of the street, just as I had imagined the days and even weeks before I began my trip.

I hadn't eaten since my 8:00 a.m. breakfast of crackers, cheese, and an apple at Dr. Flynn's home that morning. I had taken a five-mile run from his house just off the Emory campus to Lullwater Estate, which housed a beautiful nature reserve and the Emory University's president's home, where I had spent so many hours as a student decades before. In the parking lot of the nursing home, the car temperature reading said sixty-two degrees and the sun was brilliant. There was no wind.

It was 1:15 p.m., and I had to decide whether to wait for Diane or go in myself. In my shoulder bag I had ten photographs and a teddy bear. The photos were of Louise and me or of Louise with other members of my family or

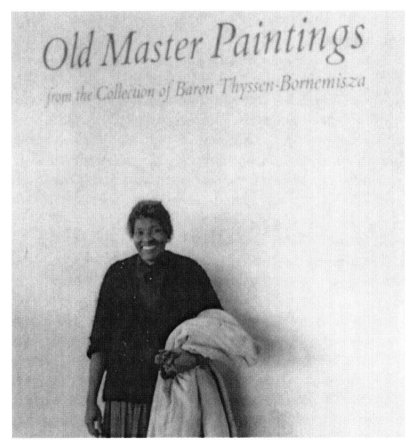

Louise at the National Gallery of Art in Washington, DC, circa 1977.

members of the neighborhood where we all lived in Somerset or Bethesda. The first photo I thought I would show her, slightly out of focus, dated from the summer of 1961, a full fifty-one years from the date of our reunion. There was Louise standing behind a group of neighborhood kids and myself on our lawn in Somerset, Maryland. Other photos were of Louise in front of our Bethesda home or Louise in the home or Louise in front of and in the National Gallery of Art in Washington, DC. One of my favorites shows her standing under a marquee of an exhibit entitled "Master Painters" with her so well-dressed and elegant in the bright sunlight, her brilliant smile dominating the scene.

I could not bear to wait any longer as I walked from the car to the front door of the nursing home. "Better to charge ahead than to wait" my emotions told me, like a boy who knew he had to get vaccination at the pediatrician's office. The nursing home director's door was just past the entrance on the left, and it was ajar. I knocked and introduced myself, announcing with some degree of pride that I was here to see someone I hadn't seen in thirty-one years. After briefly explaining my purpose and showing the director some photos, she elicited the characteristic reactions I heard from so many people who had heard my story in the weeks and months prior: admiration, curiosity, and a sense of awe. She informed me of Louise's room number and had an assistant lead me there.

"Louise Johnson Morris" read the small plastic nameplate outside her room. We knocked and waited as I tried to control my breathing. Hearing nothing, we entered slowly to find the room empty. "She must be in the lunchroom," the assistant said. I took a deep breath and followed her down the hall, the teddy bear clutched under my arm. "Dante's

Inferno" I thought, as I glanced at the sick and elderly, wheelchair-bound residents strewn like so many stones along a riverbank. One old black woman, listing to one side in her chair, absently clutched a Cabbage Patch doll. "Don't dare try to take her baby," the assistant blurted. "Ain't nobody going to take that baby," she insisted.

The lunchroom was spacious and held ten or so large tables where the residents sat dining along with their spoon-feeding caretakers. "Where's Louise?" I asked, my eyes scanning the room. "Over yonder in the back, under the pink blanket."

After more than three decades, the moment had come. "How could that be Weezy?" I thought. A young African American woman sat to her left, spoon-feeding oatmeal that overflowed from Weezy's mouth. I took a position to the right of Louise's wheelchair, her legs extended out long and her arms out to the side. I searched her face intently, trying to recognize vestiges of the woman who had raised me my entire childhood. Her eyes were downcast, and her lower lip was swollen and covered in oatmeal. But it was the nose and high cheekbones, so similar to her son Chester's, that gave it away. The expression struck me as one I had seen recently. Yes! So eerily similar to the Christian Savior's face in the famous "lost" painting "The Taking of Christ" by the master Caravaggio. (The painting has its own story and book called *The Lost Painting*. It was procured for almost nothing by an Irish doctor, and she left it in her will to a Jesuit Home in Dublin. When the paintings there were in need of cleaning, the restorer, to his astonishment, discovered that the work, misattributed to another lesser painter, was actually Caravaggio's lost masterpiece and was worth forty million dollars.)

"Weezy," I said, "it's me, Davis. Do you remember me? You raised me." I placed the teddy bear gently on her lap and handed the caregiver the pictures I had brought with me. "I haven't seen this woman in thirty-one years," I exclaimed, with a mixture of pride and self-consciousness. Some of the other caretakers gathered around to look at the photographs, admiring how beautiful Louise appeared in earlier days. Weezy remained silent.

"Weezy," I continued, "it's me. Remember Daniel, Lisa, and Debbie?" citing the names of my siblings.

"Yes, ma'am," she replied in a wavering and low voice.

"No, Louise, I'm not a ma'am. It's me, Davis. I love you!"

"I love you, too," she responded.

Not sure I was making the connection, I looked at the caregiver with frustration. "I'd better let her finish lunch," I said, my own stomach growling. My watch read 1:25 p.m. I had thirty-five minutes until Diane arrived, and I figured I'd get something to eat and come back to the nursing home around 2:00 p.m.

Stepping back into the Macon sunshine, I scanned the horizon for a place to get food. Prospects were bleak: a Popeye's fried chicken, a mini mart, and the bakery. The bakery proved closed. Popeye's was out of the question. All I could think of was what got most of these Southerners sick from hypertension, diabetes, and heart disease. I entered the mini mart. A man of Asian-Indian descent worked furtively behind the bulletproof glass. Coffee yes, but no milk. Only the artery clogging powder stuff. I poured some black coffee and searched for something real to eat ~ an apple, banana, anything. No such luck. I finally decided on a bag of pistachios, paid the man, and took my "lunch" outside.

No place to sit. I walked to the bakery's parking lot and planted my butt on the concrete parking space stop. Sipping a coffee and shelling the pistachios, I chewed and drank, discarding the shells on the ground. "At least these pistachios are natural," I thought. A black teenager, his pants halfway down his ass with a baseball cap sideways, crossed the parking lot, not giving me a look. It was 1:55 p.m. Time to get back. I spat out a final pistachio shell and rose to my feet.

I climbed up the hill, reentered the nursing home, and found Diane in the lobby. We had obviously never met, but we knew each other instantly; me by my age, race, and appearance and she by her family resemblance to the Johnsons. Accompanying her was her daughter, Yolanda, and ten-year-old granddaughter, the adorable and bespectacled Chastity.

After some stilted hellos, we walked the short distance to Weezy's room. There sat Louise, teddy bear in her lap, her head down and her body slumped to the right.

"Look who's come to see you, Aunt Louise!" Diane exclaimed. "Dr. Scheer, the boy you raised."

I bent over and kissed Weezy's forehead. Again, her voice was weak and low. I spread the photos in her lap as Diane and the others marveled at the decades-old images of their beloved relative. Over the course of the next hour, we shared stories and photos about Louise that Diane had saved from the time after Louise had moved back to Macon. A general commotion ensued as more relatives, caretakers, and nursing home workers came in and out of the room to witness the scene. I began to feel slightly embarrassed, feeling like both rock star and prodigal son, when sister-in-law Dottie entered with her daughter Cheryl.

Dottie was Louise's brother Frank's wife ~ elegant, tall, and dressed to the nines. I surmised she had just come from church. I had heard much about Frank from Chester a month before when we had dinner in Baltimore ~ how he was a young, strapping Marine as a young man, made good in Macon, met President Clinton and Coretta Scott King, carried the Olympic torch through Macon on its way to Atlanta in 1996, and was feted for his achievements by the NAACP. He'd even had a recreation center named after him in Macon.

All of us spoke as if we were family, my recanting stories of Louise's life from 1961 to 1981 and the family opening up her life to me in the time surrounding those dates. I had brought my camera from DC, and Chastity was eager to act as an able photographer. Not wanting to tire Louise out, Dottie asked me if I'd like to take a break and visit the farm where Louise grew up as well as the "Home-House" where she was born and the surrounding houses on the ten siblings were born and raised. She also asked me if I wanted to meet her husband, Frank. I replied that I was eager to meet him and see these places described so many times by Louise in my childhood.

I told Louise I loved her, kissed her on the forehead, and left with the group for the parking lot.

Cheryl drove Dottie, Chastity, and me in the white Cadillac. Dottie insisted I sit in the front. The Johnson farm, recently sold by the family, was a mere five minutes' drive from the nursing home. Cheryl pulled the car over to the curb as I, at long last, laid eyes and set foot on a piece of earth I had heard about since early childhood. This patch of land, inherited by descendants of southern slaves, was hallowed ground, I thought. This is where Louise worked as

The Johnson Farm in Macon, Georgia. Louise worked the land on this hallowed ground, rendered as reparation for slavery.

a child and young woman, helped her parents scratch out a living, and developed her almost superhuman strength and work ethic. A lone sign stood at the front of the property facing the street. It read: "Johnson Farm." I shook my head in wonder and snapped some pictures. Quick images of Louise pushing a plow hit my brain.

It was time to move across the street to the "Home-House." We drove for two minutes perpendicular to the farm and came upon a hardscrabble patch of land dotted with small homes. The largest, a purple, wooden frame house, was where all the Johnson children were born. We got out of the car. A tabby cat immediately came up and brushed my ankle. "That's my baby," Cheryl exclaimed. She then pointed out a simple wooden bench on the lawn where Louise would sit on temperate mornings to soak up the sunshine.

Dottie explained the layout of the property as I absorbed the very historic and personal significance of this place. Cheryl remarked how one of the dogs had been found last week with a dead cat in his mouth. "Fortunately," she remarked, "my baby's too fast for that dog." Time was getting on, and Dottie suggested we all take the short minute drive to visit Frank at his nursing home.

We returned to pick up my rental car from Heritage Healthcare, and I then followed the family to the Cherry Blossom nursing home where Frank lived. Cherry Blossom was much like Heritage Healthcare, both in appearance and clientele. In just a short time, I was led to Frank's room. There he sat, his back to the door, watching television, his gray head of hair full and fluffy. The once strapping Marine, as evidenced by pictures of him sixty years gone by, now sat in a wheelchair, a double amputee. I was introduced to him by Dottie and realized that this was the only sibling of Louise's I had ever met. Searching his face for any family resemblance, I saw Louise's high cheekbones and proud, prominent nose.

Dottie led me on a tour of Frank's shrine, a collection of two dozen or so photographs and newspaper clippings spanning his life. One showed Frank jogging and carrying the Olympic torch in 1996. Another revealed him with Coretta Scott King and another with Bill Clinton. My favorite, however, showed him as a young Marine with five or six black comrades; he stood front and center ~ tall, proud, strong. I wondered what it must've been like to be a black soldier in the mid-twentieth century ~ the hardships, the prejudice, the bond between black brothers necessary to keep one's dignity and even safety. The experience left me deeply moved.

Perhaps Dottie's greatest pride was the photo of the dedication of the Frank Johnson Recreation Center in Macon. Frank had been so vital and instrumental to the quality of life in this corner of Macon that this honor was well-deserved. I shook Frank's hand again and, after some small talk, indicated to Dottie that the time was getting late, and I probably should be getting back to Atlanta for dinner with my host, Dr. Flynn. I said my goodbyes to Frank and then the family, thanking them for this gift of the day, a day so long overdue. Louise's ninetieth birthday would be seven weeks away, and I offered up the possibility of a repeat visit in early spring.

All of us embraced and I got into the car, relieved that I had survived the last four hours without breaking down. Diane led me out to I-85 in her car and, as she pointed the exit out, I gave her a wave and reflected on the day and whether I'd ever see Louise again. The drive back to Atlanta was sunny and silent. After trying to digest the day's events, I was looking forward to a stiff drink at the home of Dr. Flynn.

Chapter Ten

Celestial House

ॐ

Naples, Florida and Macon, Georgia
April 5th and 14th, 2012

We were on spring break, Laura, Liam, and I. The night was beautiful and unusually warm for southwest Florida this time of year. I had made dinner reservations at a sidewalk Italian bistro on Fifth Avenue for 7:00 p.m. As the hostess was leading us to our table, my cell phone rang. It was Diane, Louise's niece. I recognized the voice instantly ~ she always called me Dr. Sheer. I gave her a cheerful greeting, as I always did, but she told me she had bad news. "We just lost our Louise," she said, sadness and resignation in her voice. I felt as if I had been kicked in the gut. Just as I was offering my condolences, Chester was ringing in on call waiting. I let that go, and I continued to speak with Diane. "What happened?" I asked. She told me that the last two days, Louise was not talking, eating or drinking much, and just today she had rallied a bit. When Diane had come in to see Louise she thought she was asleep. The caretaker came in and told Diane, "God, I'm so sorry." Diane asked, "What do you mean?" "Louise passed away about fifteen minutes ago," he replied.

"What are the arrangements?" I asked Diane, and she said she didn't know, but she would be sure to tell me when. She also said that the family would like me to say a few words at the service. I told her I would be honored to and to keep me updated on the situation. I then called Chester to tell him how sorry I was. He took it pretty well, and we agreed to keep in touch and coordinate on the funeral timing. After goodbyes, I sat down and told Laura that Louise had just died and that I might have to fly to Atlanta within the next few days. Laura laid her hand on my arm and told me how badly she felt for me.

Just then, a gay couple, two white men in their thirties, walked out of the restaurant, weaving among the patio diners, one of them carrying a baby basket with a small black girl, probably six months old. One life had just left the planet and another was beginning. I turned to Laura and remarked, "I'd give just about anything to know that baby's name. I wonder if it could be Louise."

###

Saturday, April 14, 2012

I awoke at 4:00 a.m. after not having slept well. As usual, I had over-packed for my planned three days in Georgia with formal clothes for the funeral and workout gear I knew I would need to clear my mind. By 4:30 a.m., I had headed out the door and began the drive through the deathly quiet streets of Chevy Chase and onto Connecticut Avenue toward the Washington Beltway. At that hour, the land is like a big organism: quiet residential streets like capillaries, busier avenues like veins, and, finally, the heart-like clover leaf gives way to the aortic Beltway, already busy with cars. "Where could these people possibly be going at this hour?" I wondered.

I got the car parked in the daily lot by 5:00 a.m. at Reagan National Airport. The security line was short and, incredibly, by 5:45 we were in our seats. Any plan to read a book or the morning paper was quickly vanquished as I put my chin in my open hand and dozed in and out for the eighty-minute flight. The Monopoly board that is Hartsfield-Jackson Atlanta International Airport posed its usual challenges. Fortunately, there was no need to deal with baggage claim. After I made my way past the junk food, tchotchkes, and modern-day bazaars, I hopped the train to "rental cars" and had my butt in the seat of the Nissan Versa by 8:15 a.m. The funeral in Macon was set for 1:00 p.m., and I was to meet Diane about 12:30. Exhausted as I was, that left me some time to get to Dr. Flynn's home, maybe catch a nap, and by 11:00 be on my way. It was a little after 9:00 when Tom opened the door to his home. Understanding as usual, he told me to get some rest and that we could reconnect upon my return that evening. I spent the two hours in my room dreading and fearing the day's events ahead of me.

My choice of clothing was deliberate ~ a light-colored sports jacket, khakis, a blue shirt, and a yellow tie patterned with small, bright lemons. I could not bear to wear black for I wanted to celebrate the light that Louise represented to me. On my feet were my best Johnston and Murphy brogues. After I bade Dr. Flynn goodbye, I headed toward

Interstate 75. The day was bright and the car thermometer read seventy-two degrees. The trip was a repeat of the one I took three months before when I had first reconnected with Louise on Martin Luther King, Jr. weekend. There was sparse traffic, glaring sunshine, the radio, and my thoughts. Traffic heading into Atlanta was steady. A Braves game or a road race or both, I figured. At 12:15, I called Diane on my cell phone, and we agreed to meet at the same convenience store where I had purchased my lunch of pistachios and coffee ninety days before.

I followed Diane to her house where the "Twin Towers," Chester and his son JaQuan, were easy to spot from a distance. About twenty people, all African American and all dressed in black formal wear, milled about the front yard. A white limousine sat parked by the curb.

Recognizing the familiar faces from my trip in January, I greeted Dottie, Cheryl, Chester, his wife Shanta, Chastity, and JaQuan with hugs and condolences. Chester appeared at peace; dignified, proud, handsome in his black tie. His face was noble and, as I already remarked, bore the same high cheekbones and distinctive nose that were the hallmark of his late mother. Conveying my sorrow and love all around, I was made to feel at home among friends and strangers alike.

The cameras and the iPhones clicked away as the time drew near to get to the church. "You ride with us," Chester said to me as he opened the door to the limo and I slid inside. Chester and JaQuan angled themselves into the car, their long legs bent till their knees were chin-high like ballplayers sitting on a bench. There was quiet laughter, small talk, and then silence as we approached the Bethel African Methodist Episcopal (AME) Church adjacent to the cemetery.

There we stood, about twenty-five people in all: a small knot of humanity, gathered at the front steps of the church that ascended into the nave. From an aerial shot, we would have looked like a flock of elegant, sleek ravens with a sole yellow canary at its center. There was Louise's ninety-seven-year-old sister, Carrie; thin, frail, and supported by relatives as she was led up the steps. As we deliberately and silently made our way forward, I saw Louise's open casket in front of the altar. The front row on the right was left open for family members, and I was directed to take my place there. I made my way quietly to the last seat on the right, conspicuous as the only non-African American present and the only person not wearing black. Directly, Chester got up to kiss the forehead of his mother, turned, and sat down. Without hesitation or embarrassment, I walked directly to the casket and did the same. Her forehead was like cold marble. The crowd remained silent as I returned to my seat. A few coughs and a shuffling of programs circled the room.

In my lap sat the program. As the mourners continued to come in, about fifty in all, I read the page facing the program entitled the obituary. It read: "On Thursday afternoon, April 5, 2012, our Lord and Savior Jesus Christ whispered into our beloved Louise Johnson Morris's ear and said: 'You've fought a great fight, My child. After ninety years, the battle is over. Now take My hand and come home with Me to the promised land.'

"Mrs. Louise Johnson Morris was born March 10th, 1922 in Macon, Bibb County, Georgia to the parentage of the late Mr. Thomas Baker Johnson and the late Mrs. Cherry Hilman Johnson.

"After graduating from Hudson High School, she moved to Washington, DC where she resided for many years before returning home in the mid-80s. She reunited with her home church, the Bethel AME Church, where she was a faithful member until her health failed.

"Louise never met a stranger and enjoyed talking to people and doing her 'missionary work,' as she called it. She was always willing to do whatever she could to assist family members and other people that she came in contact with. She believed in rising early and getting started on her daily tasks.

"Louise's survivors include her son, Chester (wife, Shanta) Morris, Baltimore, Maryland; reared as a son, Dr. David Sherer, Bethesda, Maryland; grandchild, JaQuan Morris; stepchildren, Shawnicey Smith and Delonta Smith; siblings, Frank (wife, Dorothy P. Johnson), Carrie J. Hughes, and Mary McDade, Philadelphia, Pennsylvania; devoted nieces, Diane (husband, Clarence J. Matthews), and Cheryl Jane Knight; and other relatives."

I glanced quickly at the program, entitled Order of Service. It was as follows: "A musical prelude; processional sung by the choir called 'Parting Glance;' A hymn, 'Oh I Want to See Him;' A prayer by the Rev. B. Darrell Walker; scripture readings: one from the Old Testament, Ecclesiastes 3:1 through 8, by Bishop Calvin Watkins, Sr.; a reading from the New Testament by the Rev. Charlie A. Hicks II; a hymn called 'Blessed Assurance;' reflections by Ms. Lillie Harvey, Dr. Mildred P. Hill, and Dr. David Sherer; a solo song by Ms. Martha Harrell; a eulogy by the Rev. Carlton Mahone, Sr.; acknowledgements and a recessional entitled 'I'll Fly Away.'" The interment was to be at Mosley Cemetery, where Louise's parents lay buried.

I had been to other African American services in the past, often so different from services of other cultures, and have marveled at the deeply expressed emotion, conviction in faith, and sheer energy of the experience. This service was no exception. I was moved by the passion of the gospel choir and the wisdom of the readings from Scripture. The Rev. Carlton Mahone, Sr., a light-skinned, African American with piercing blue eyes, directed from the altar and introduced the three speakers.

First was Ms. Lillie Harvey who had been a long-time friend of Louise's. Small, immaculately dressed, and supremely eloquent, she explained what her relationship with Louise meant to her:

"I met Louise in the mid-1980s when she had moved to start another career. After she had worked in Washington and left that area, she came home to Macon and started anew. It seemed that every day Louise would spend her time clearing the twigs and bushes around the general landscape of the Johnson Farm. When she was done with that, it seems she moved on to clearing up and down the street. [Laughter] Up and down the neighborhood, pulling broken branches, and when she was done with that, she would start cleaning up another farm. [More laughter] She spent her time babysitting her brother, Frank, which she started to do in the year 2000. If Dottie would be late to take care of Frank, Louise was sure to be there. She had a life well-lived and well-worked.

"She touched many lives, leaving an everlasting imprint on those of us who came her way. To sum it all up, her work has already spoken for her. The world would have lost a lot had she not come our way. [At that point I said out loud: 'Amen!']. Emerson said, the reward well done is to have done it. Louise has laid down her shovel and her hoe, and she picked up the fiddle and bow. There is no more work for our dear friend, Louise, for she has gone where all God's

Christians go. So may we live as she lived, and may we feel as she felt when God said 'well done.' Goodnight, Louise, we'll see you in the morning."

Ms. Harvey took her seat and Dr. Mildred Hill, Dottie's sister, spoke next, movingly and lovingly. After formal salutations to the audience, she said: "Two statements come to mind when I think of Louise: inquiring minds want to know, and, a statement, made in the book *The Help* by one of the lead characters to a little girl: 'You're smart, you're pretty, and you're important.' I want to thank Diane and my sister, Dorothy, for asking me to say a few words. It didn't take me long to formulate what I would say about Louise. Now, it was suggested that I would say that Louise is a fixture because she was always around. Louise was always around. And her favorite spot when I came to visit was on that bench. I think you know how the house is fashioned [the main "Home-House"]. The window of the kitchen does not face the entry of the house. The person in the house doesn't get to be standing in the window to see what's going on. That's why Louise was out there sitting on that bench. I would never, ever go to Dorothy's house without Louise sitting there while she was stopping in.

"Louise had an inquiring mind. She was full of questions. And whatever was on her mind that she wanted to ask me, Louise asked me those questions, and I was not going to get in that place until I answered those questions. Louise was very smart, too. And she loved people. I was not going to get into that house until she told me how pretty I was and how smart I was. According to Louise, there would be no one prettier than me. And there wasn't anybody smarter. She said, 'You know, I've been around a heap of people, and they ain't as smart as you, and I don't care how many beautiful folks they got in Hollywood, they don't look good as you.' [Laughter] That was Louise. And every day, whenever I saw Louise, she would tell me that. This is where I'm going, Rev. Mahone. You might not have gotten to know Louise real well, and I can't say, but Louise made it her business to have a conversation with the Lord to find out just how things are. You know: 'Tell me Lord, I want to know,' and I can tell you she asked Him some specific questions. [More laughter] And I believe He answered her questions. I can also imagine that Louise not only asked the Lord some questions, but she told God some things as well. 'You know, Lord, I've been going to church and they said this and they said that, and I believe that You know somebody said something and I want to ask You: What you think about that?' [Rev. Mahone says: "My, my, my." Laughter.] I can imagine that. And finally, the thing that really warms my heart is that I believe that our spirits will meet again. ['Praise God' from the crowd] And I believe that Louise loved people. Louise would come to my house. Louise would say, 'You know this is the prettiest place I ever seen,' and she would look and she could pick out things and now I believe that Louise is at the Throne, checking everything out [that was SO Louise], and she would want us to know just what they said; not only what it is like, but that it is better than that. 'Lord, you know I'm going to have a good time up here.' And, Louise, guess what ~ I want to get there to share it with you! Amen."

Then it was my turn to speak. Unprepared, rambling, awkward, and shooting from the hip and heart, I began: "Thank all of you. I may to appear to be an outsider, but I'm not an outsider. Louise came into my life when I was eighteen months old. She raised me, often at the expense of her own son. Those were the days and still are the days when black men and women had to sacrifice. Why? Because they were looked down upon in our society. That was a disgrace. They were brought to this country in slavery, which to me, next to the murder of people, is the greatest sin that can be committed. [Amen!] Any person who would enslave another person because of the color of their skin, their beliefs, religion has committed a great evil. And so, I learned from Louise many things in my life, and I became a changed person. I learned of the suffering of black people in the United States. I learned that the work of Dr. King and Rosa Parks would not go in vain.

"As I grew up in Somerset and Bethesda, Louise became at times more of a mother to me than, I daresay, my own mother. I love my mother, I loved my father, but Louise was always there for me. And she taught me so many things about a culture that I would have never known. She gave me so many gifts, I could never repay her in a hundred lifetimes. She told me funny things. She told me how people speak in Macon. [Laughter] She told me how she grew up on the farm. How she would push the plow. She told me 'ain't nobody perfect but God.' She told me 'you can't tell the seasons but for the buddin' of trees.' Sometimes she'd be so cold waiting for us to pick her up at the District Line that her teeth would 'pop together.' She would say things like 'mind your own business; you got your own shorts on ain't cha'? [More laughter]

"I went to college here in Georgia, at Emory. I had other possibilities, I could have gone other places, but I knew that Louise's sister, Susie Sublett, lived on Sunset Avenue, and one of the first things I did was to call Susie because I want to learn about this family of seven girls and three boys. Well, to make a long story short, I went off to medical school, and

I saw and reflected how well Louise took care of me and my three siblings and even my grandmother. And then something happened. She left our home under circumstances I don't really understand, but I don't particularly care what the circumstances were. And then I got busy in life, practicing medicine, raising a family, doing things that grownups do, and I turned past my middle age and I thought to myself: 'What's important in my life?' And I was ashamed. I was ashamed because I hadn't made the effort I should have made to find this beautiful, wise, generous woman. The best way I could describe Louise? She was the Real Deal Holy Field! There was nothing pretentious about Louise, nothing fake. What you see was you got. ['That's right!' from the crowd.] There were never any airs, never any 'I'm better than you,' but she did say once, when she was watching TV with me, she said about President Nixon: 'That man don't look good as my foot! [Peals of laughter] I wish the Kennedy mens was in the chair again.' [Laughter]

"So I decided I want to find this beautiful woman. Back in the 80s there was no Internet and cell phones were not popular or commonly used. Places to research and try to find people were not as prevalent, so last year, on the 150th anniversary of the start of the Civil War, I said to myself, 'The waiting is over.' I am going to find her. So I started with the only link I could think of, which was Chester. I started to make Internet inquiries about Chester Lee Morris. And I found Chester and I found the blessing that Louise was still alive at the age of ninety. So the first thing I did I booked a flight as soon as I could and met her and her beautiful family and I saw my Louise alive for the last time. I give my deepest condolences from my family to your family." I stepped down from the altar and sat down.

###

The mourners proceeded slowly out of the church and into the midday sunshine. The casket (the funeral industry never allows the use of the word "coffin") was carried by pallbearers to the awaiting hearse. The drive was short since the cemetery is adjacent to the church. As the group gathered around, waiting for all the attendees, I took note of the headstones in the ground. Astounded at the link to history upon where I stood, I read the tombstones of Louise's parents, the children of slaves:

Cherry Johnson

Louise's father grave marker. Note the birth year, 1874, a mere nine years after the close of the American Civil War.

Born Dec. 25, 1888
Died Apr. 11, 1967

Thomas B. Johnson
Born Feb. 8, 1874
Died Feb. 8, 1934

Eighteen seventy-four! I was humbled. Here was living, breathing history under my very feet. The man was born a mere nine years after the end of the bloodiest conflict in our nation's history! Like the direct link I had to Beethoven from the lineage of Nadia Boulanger and Anthony Chanaka, this connection afforded me the privilege of being part of another piece of history. I had read William Tecumseh Sherman's and Ulysses S. Grant's seminal autobiographies in the prior months, learning about the "forty acres and a mule" dictum that allotted newly freed slaves a way to get on their feet, but to see the Johnson Farm, meet these wonderful and welcoming descendants, and see these remnants of that time was overwhelming. The entire experience ~ the funeral, the new friendship, the honoring of a "life well-lived" ~ was not a gift from me to the Johnson family. Quite truthfully, it was the other way around.

Afterword

๛

Aside from same sex marriage, abortion, and the role of the federal government in our lives, perhaps the most polarizing issue we face today in the United States is that of race. A full century and a half after the start of the Civil War, the lingering effects of that catastrophic conflict is felt every day in our nation. Despite gradual improvement and reform in the treatment and rights of African Americans, the stain of slavery, I believe, will take decades, perhaps even a century or more, to resolve.

In all the years that I knew her, Louise and I rarely got into discussing the subject of race. It wasn't for lack of opportunity for there was ample time she and I spent together discussing a variety of topics. Having come from the Deep South, Louise must have experienced racism in its most basic and even brutal forms. You could not have been black in the South in the early half of the twentieth century and not felt the sting of prejudice.

The Civil Rights Act of 1964, brought to fruition by President Lyndon Johnson and Martin Luther King, Jr., among others, did much to bring the law and the spirit of the law toward more racial equality in many areas of public life. But, as laws are subject to interpretation, they can be molded, massaged, or disregarded altogether, often under the guise of "states' rights" or, more overtly, in outright challenge to their constitutionality.

My early life with Louise as caregiver, role model, and even sometime surrogate mother fell amidst this volcanic civil rights upheaval. I was merely seven years old when the 1964 Act came along, and the years of my childhood straddled the times when blacks felt the full brunt of "Jim Crow," and onward through the remarkably gutsy actions of Malcolm X, the radical activities of the Black Panthers, and the non-violent efforts of Martin Luther King, Jr. In subsequent years, some semblance of maturation in America's view of race relations took hold. Unfortunately, for Louise, a smart but relatively uneducated, almost destitute black woman from Georgia, it was too little too late for her to realize much benefit from what her brethren struggled so hard to achieve.

When I tell this story to people, many ask me if Louise really recognized me after our decades-long separation. Her poor health and difficulty speaking clearly made it hard for me to discern, while I was with her, whether she truly did remember me. I was glad to hear, however, that ensuing discussions between Louise, Dottie, Cheryl, and Diane about my family and me included many references to the old times. They all laughed about how Louise fixated on making a "combination salad" for my lunch.

###

My sister, Lisa, died in December of 1982. She had had enough of diabetes, which by that time had made her blind, neuropathic, weak, and with a failed kidney transplant. As I mentioned earlier, she had gotten a lawyer, documented her wishes and intentions, and stopped taking her insulin. She died within three days.

My brother, Daniel, earned his B.A. in art history at Yale, studied at Cambridge in England, was a James B. Duke fellow at Duke University, earned his Ph.D. in art history at Harvard, and now teaches the history of architecture at Columbia, Yale, and Cooper Union.

My father died in 2007 at the age of 87 after practicing medicine for almost fifty-six years. He played golf up until the year he died.

My sister, Deb, is an artist in Bethesda and takes care of our mother in our childhood home.

My grandmother died in the late 1970s.

My uncle has retired to Philadelphia.

Chester and his family live in a Baltimore suburb.

JaQuan is at college in Oklahoma, playing under a basketball scholarship.

My mother is my mother.

At this writing, my mother is eighty-five years old and living in the family's Bethesda home where she has resided for fifty-one years. We talk by phone almost every day, and I visit her on weekends, often with my son, Liam.

Mom and I share an uneasy but enduring détente. She has a great memory for the remote past and is quick to tell stories of ancestors and the old times in Palestine,

Philadelphia, New York, Silver Spring, Somerset, and Bethesda. We talk of old friends and characters we knew, our times as piano partners, and the strengths and foibles of friends and family members. She loves to hear me imitate people we know and have known. She calls my handsome son "Czarevich," roughly translated, by her, as "little czar."

I have tried to temper my anger and frustration over her caustic relationship with my father and the general strife that went on in our family. My approach with her is one of detached understanding: I want to try and learn why she feels and felt the way she does about our collective lives, all the while realizing that there are three sides to every story: her version, my version, and the truth.

She is insistent, however, that my father caused her a lot of misery and heartache. She maintains that he never liked himself, never succeeded as much as he could have if he had more ambition, and was most certainly the cause of her devastating back injury. She dwells on the tragedy of Lisa's death and the sadness it caused us. She professes remorse about her version of the story that compelled Louise to leave the family (that Louise allegedly stole from the family and had to be taken away by the Montgomery County Police), but she sticks to it. Like a dog gnawing at a bone, she obsesses on what "might have been," seemingly not able to move on and take each day as it comes.

Recently, I tried a Socratic approach with Mom:

"So, Mom, why were you so angry with Dad?"

"Well, you know. He always put me down, especially in front of other people. That's because he didn't like himself. He was lazy, too. In Somerset, he'd sleep until noon and then drag himself in the office. He also didn't get Daniel from running into the street when I told him to! That's why I have him to blame for my back."

"I know he could be tough. No doubt."

"Tough. Yeah. And a bastard. Did you know when I was in going into labor with you, he was watching that movie, *The Blue Angel*?"

"You mean with Marlene Dietrich?"

"That's right. I told him, 'Max, I'm ready. We need to go to the hospital now!' But he ignored me. Kept on watching the movie. I had to get Bob and Loretta to take me down to GW so you could be born."

"Yeah, you've told me that before. Anyway, Ma, I want to ask you a question. Let's assume Dad was lazy and lacking ambition and all that. Why was that so bad?"

"Why?" she says, incredulously with widening eyes. "Because he could have made more money, had so much more, instead of staying in bed and playing so much golf!"

"Okay. But let's assume that's all true. But listen to this. Did he not work and support the family? Provide a beautiful and comfortable home? Hire Louise to cook, clean, and care for the kids? Did he not pay for piano lessons for me and Deb and Danny, camp for all the kids, vacations for all of us, put four children through college and graduate schools, all the while knowing his daughter was going to die early and him suffering with tic? Didn't you have furs, jewelry, all the clothes you could want, tickets to Kennedy Center for recitals, theater, and the symphony? Didn't he buy the land in Manassas [our farm, one of four properties we owned there] in the hopes of making a killing and having the family prospering and secure? Didn't he bust his ass every day listening to patients' problems, coming home dog-tired and having all of us always making demands on him? Didn't he? Huh?"

Mom answers with the same inflection she used to have at the pediatrician's office, "I DON'T know!"

"Well, Mom. As Weezy always said, 'Work is good for the mind.'"

And to that and her, I always tip my hat.

David Sherer
Chevy Chase, Maryland
November 23rd, 2013

CPSIA information can be obtained at www.ICGtesting.com
Printed in the USA
LVOW11s1715240516

489755LV00005B/231/P